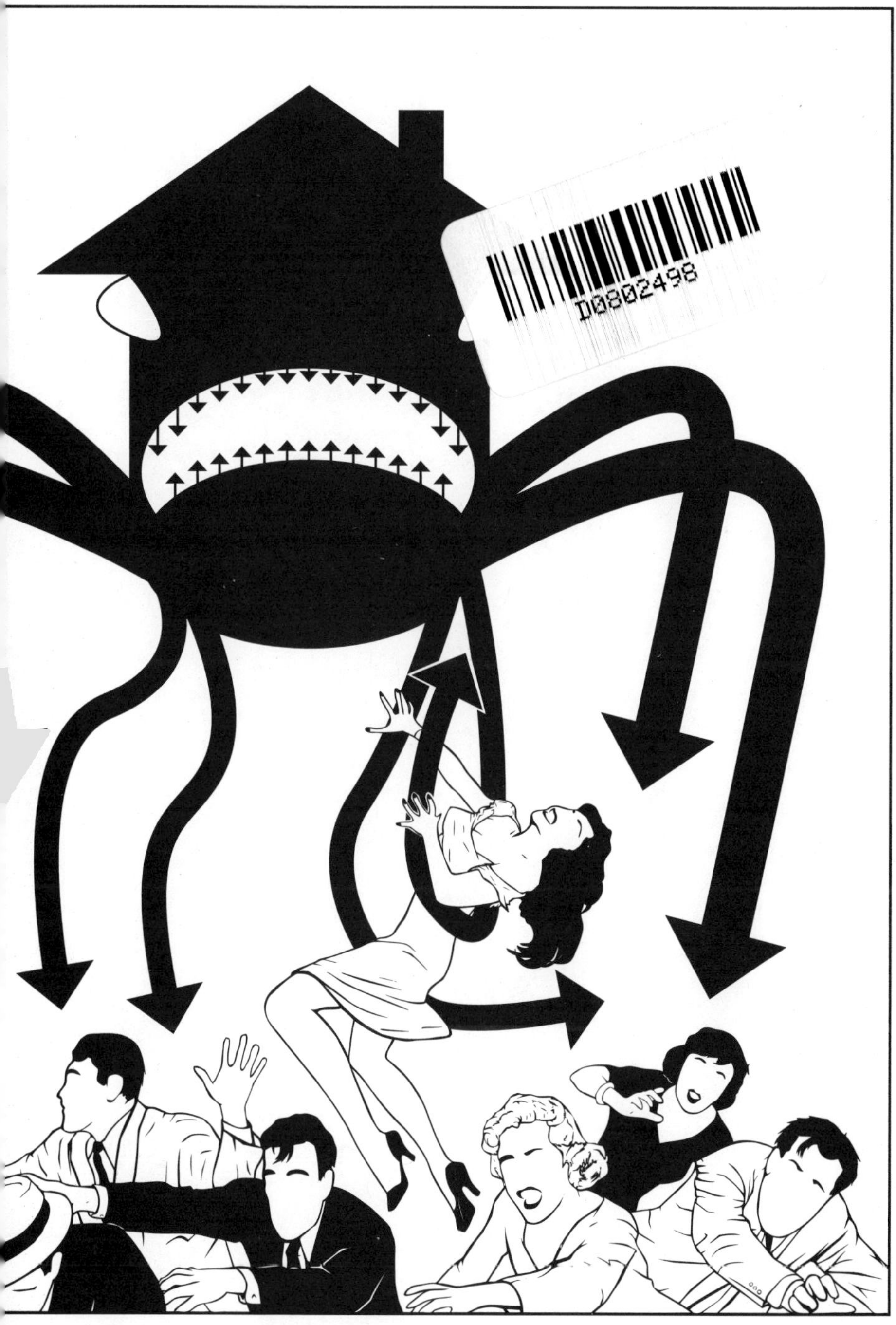

the housing monster

prole.info

the housing monster

prole.info

Editor's note: *Gender-specific words ("he," "his," "guy," etc.) are used intentionally here in relation to construction workers, contractors, owners, and so on, as an acknowledgment and critique of the status quo of pervasive sexism in a male-dominated business.*

The Housing Monster
Prole.info

PM Press
PO Box 23912
Oakland, CA 94623
www.pmpress.org

ISBN: 978-1-60486-530-1
Library of Congress Control Number: 2011939685
10 9 8 7 6 5 4 3 2 1

Printed in the USA on recycled paper, by the Employee Owners of Thomson-Shore in Dexter, Michigan.
www.thomsonshore.com

the housing monster

"We may call such a monster the 'beast of property.'
It now rules the world, making mankind miserable,
and gains in cruelty and voracity with the progress
of our so-called 'civilization.' This monster we will
in the following characterize and recommend to extermination."

Johann Most

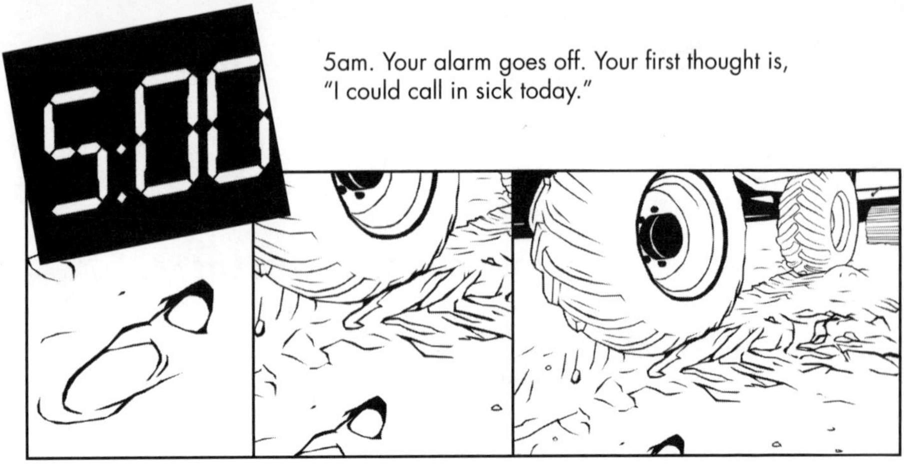
5:00

5am. Your alarm goes off. Your first thought is, "I could call in sick today."

6am. You shake yourself back awake. Outside your car window, construction workers in various degrees of consciousness are stumbling across deep backhoe tracks in the mud. It's time to go to work.

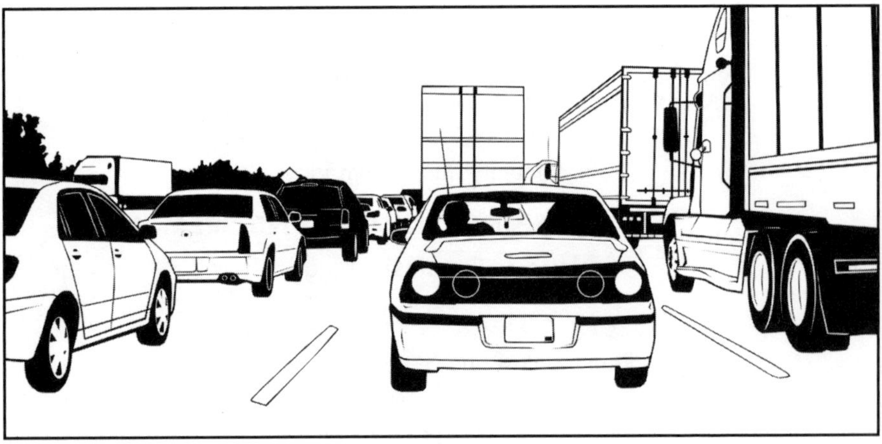

3pm. You've been in the car for 45 minutes. The traffic is terrible. A professionally neutral voice comes over the radio...

"Was the coverage of the election fair? Does the media focus too much on slips of the tongue and miss the big picture? We want to know what you have to say..."

You change the station.

"...What I don't understand is why the rioters were attacking their own neighborhood..."

You turn the radio off.

3:30. Yellow afternoon light streams through the supermarket parking lot. At the edge, an old man is sleeping on a piece of cardboard in a bus shelter. No one is sitting on the bench, but it's thin and ribbed and impossible to lie down on.

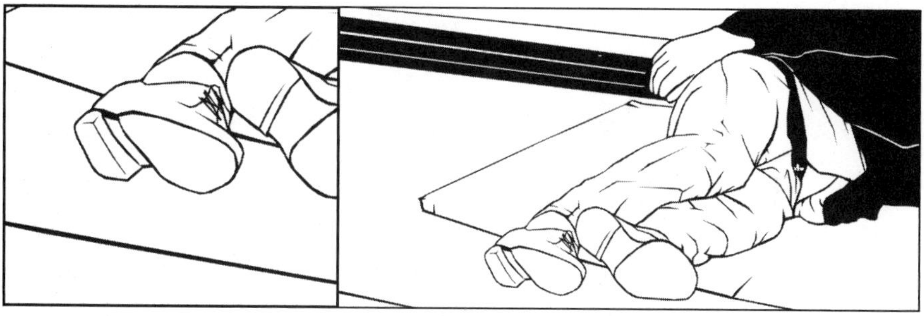

3:45. In line at the checkout, you're staring at the ground and the contents of the basket of the woman in front of you. She's buying frozen pizza, canned soup, a bottle of vitamins, and a women's magazine whose cover reads, in big bold letters: "How to Meet Mr. Right!" The only sound for several minutes is the electronic popping as the cashier scans items, takes payment, and repeats...

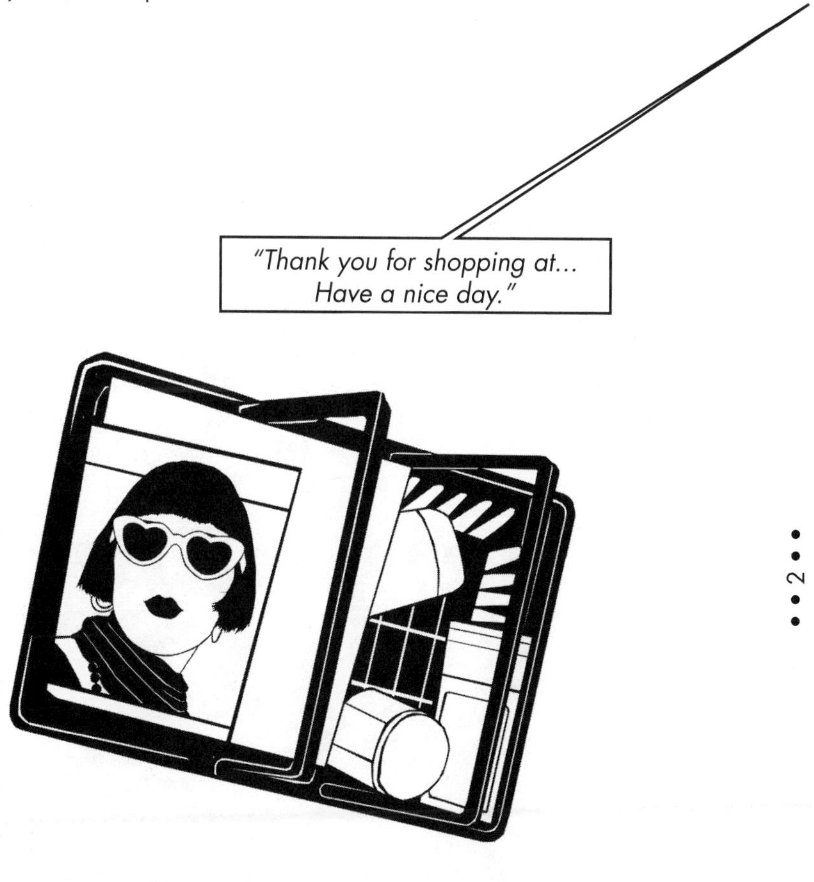
"Thank you for shopping at... Have a nice day."

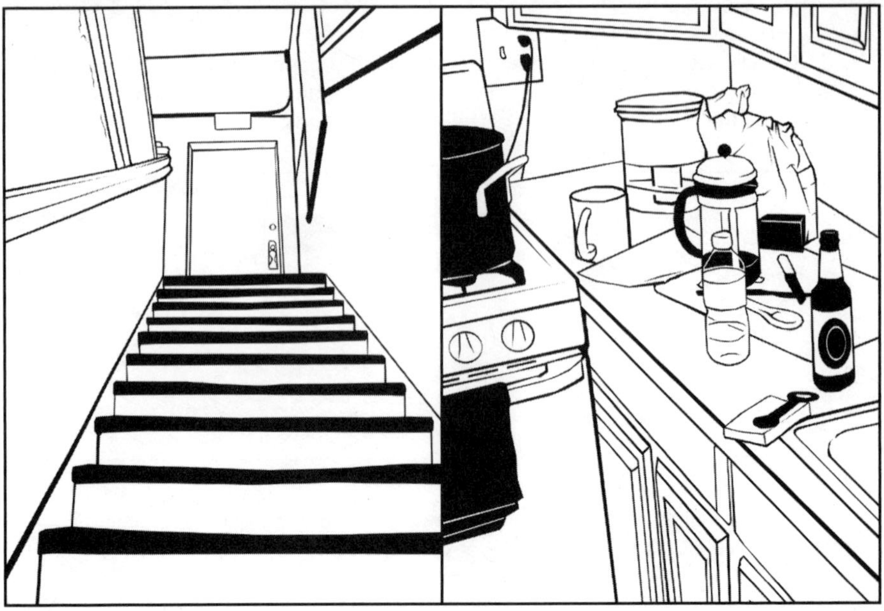

3:55. As you climb the stairs to your place, you realize how bad your knees hurt. God, you need a beer!

4:30. You're taking a shower. You sneeze and a mixture of blood and dark gray grainy stuff comes out. What is that...cement dust? Wood chips? Insulation?

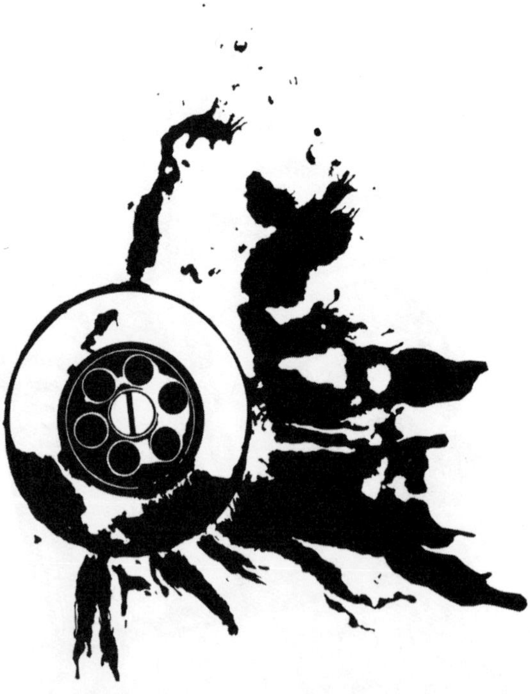

7:00. You finish eating dinner. You think about doing your laundry but decide it can wait. You're tired.

10:45. A door slams loudly and wakes you up. One of your neighbors and his teenage daughter start screaming at each other... You hear them often enough, but you've never actually spoken to them. You stare out the window at the rain in front of a streetlight. For some reason all your problems seem terrible at the moment. Oh shit, and the electric bill is due this week. You have to remember to pay that or there will be late fees.

Midnight. A neighborhood away, a house burns. The landlord has neglected the place for years. The city has strong controls on rent increases and protection against eviction. It's not clear if the fire was arson or faulty electrical wiring. What is clear is that the landlord will now be able to rebuild or renovate it and rent it out for triple the price.

A house is more than four walls and a roof. From its design and production to the way it is sold, used, resold, and eventually demolished, it is crisscrossed by conflict. From the construction site to the neighborhood, impersonal economic forces and very personal conflicts grow out of each other. Concrete, rebar, wood, and nails. Frustration, anger, resentment, and despair. Individual tragedies reflect a larger social tragedy.

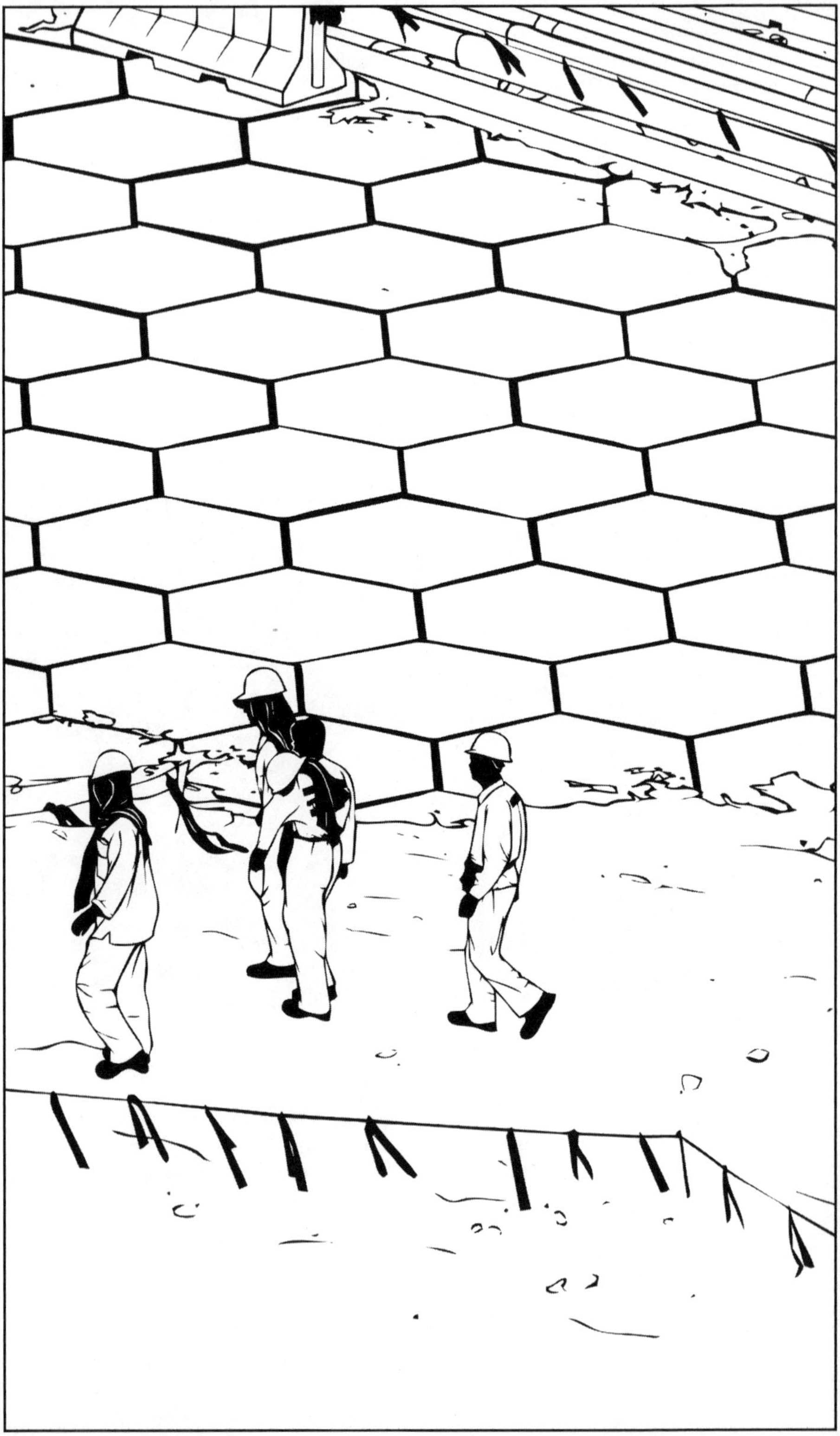

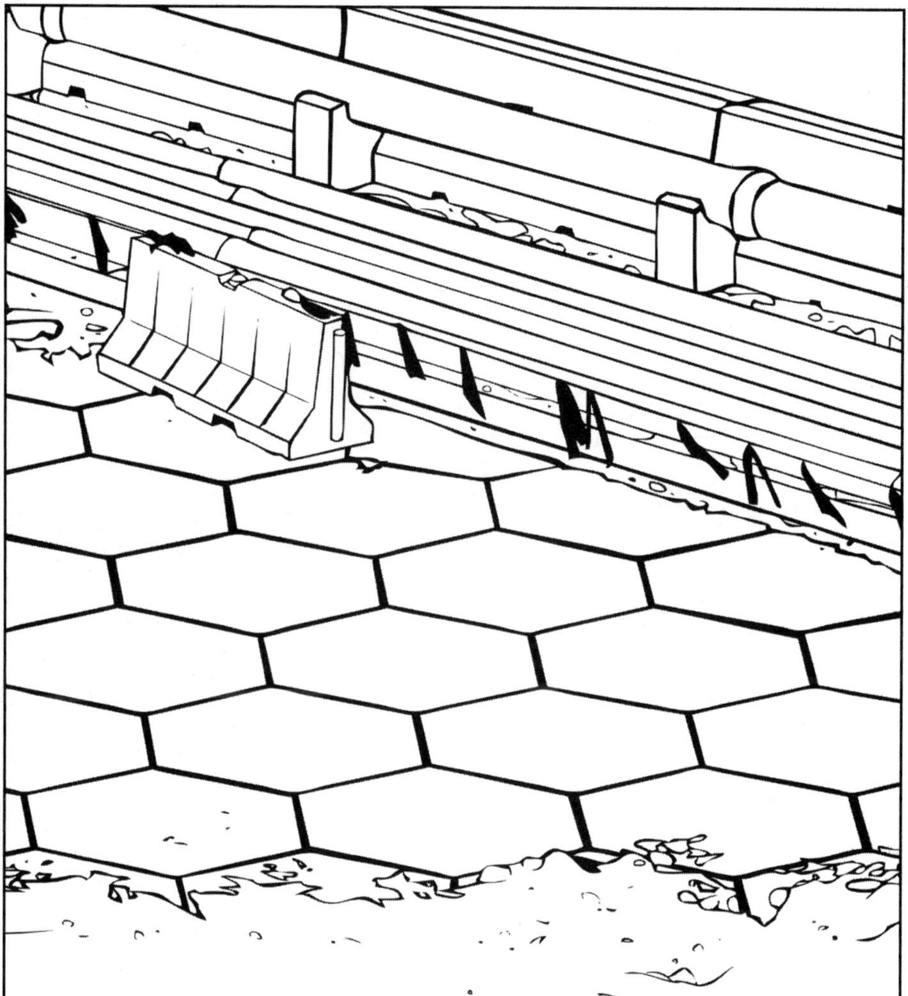

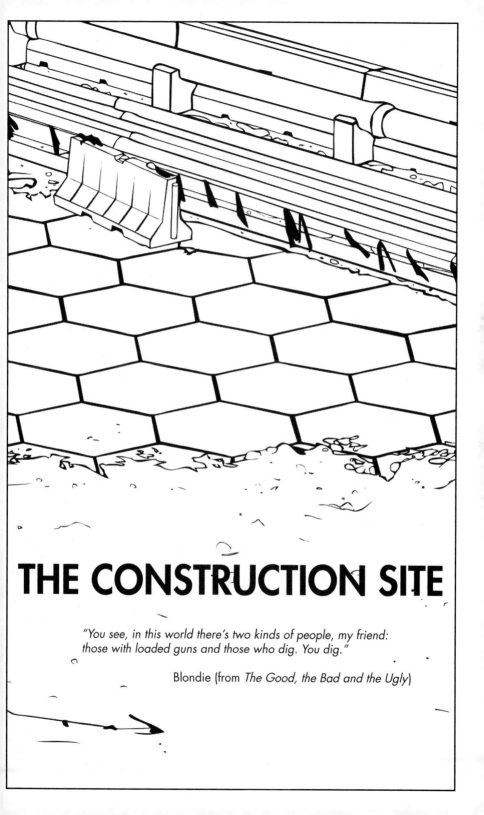

THE CONSTRUCTION SITE

"You see, in this world there's two kinds of people, my friend: those with loaded guns and those who dig. You dig."

Blondie (from *The Good, the Bad and the Ugly*)

Living and Dead Labor

"Political economy is not a science of the relation of things to things, as was thought by vulgar economists, nor of people to things, as was asserted by the theory of marginal utility, but of the relations of people to people in the process of production."

Isaak Illich Rubin

When we think of a house, we think of a physical structure meant to protect us from the weather and give us some privacy. It can have various characteristics. It can be a single-family suburban bungalow with a lawn and garage, a dark apartment in the basement of a block of brick row houses, a room halfway up a reinforced concrete housing tower, a trailer by the edge of town, a sprawling mansion by the beach with a tennis court and heated pool.

As physical structures, different kinds of houses are worth different amounts. The value of any one of them appears to be another characteristic of the house, just like whether or not it has a garage or working smoke detectors. On the basis of this value they are interchangeable. One mansion by the beach might have the same value as ten suburban houses and fifty basement apartments. Value, the thing they have in common, is not a measure of their usefulness.

The fact that a mansion (as a physical structure) is worth fifty times more money than a basement apartment, is not because it provides fifty times more shelter or fifty times more privacy or because it has 25 working smoke detectors to the basement apartment's single smoke detector that works half the time. This is even more clear when a house is compared to other commodities, like a luxury car or a box of pasta. A basement apartment might be worth half as much as a luxury car and thousands of times what a box of pasta is worth. But it would be completely ridiculous to say that this is because a basement apartment provides half as much protection from the weather and privacy as a luxury car provides ability to get from place to place quickly and in style—or that people living in the basement apartment value the shelter their apartment provides several thousand times more than they value the ability of the pasta to be turned into a tasty dinner.

If a mansion is worth ten times what a single family bungalow is worth, it's because it takes ten times as much work to make one. If it takes a specific mix of construction workers six months to build the bungalow, it would take the same workers 5 years to build the mansion, or if the mansion needed to be built in 6 months, it would take ten times as many workers. The ratios in which different types of houses could be exchanged is based on the amount of labor time that is necessary to make them (where the skilled laborer's time is worth more than the unskilled laborer's).

Commodities are produced by separate specialized enterprises. Houses and X-rays are created by completely different work processes and have completely different uses. Still X-ray technicians need houses and construction workers often need X-rays taken. Value appears as the thing that makes a social relation between them possible—it links the activity of separate commodity producers. The products of their work can be exchanged for definite amounts of money, which can then be used to buy any other commodity.

Value attaches itself to useful things, and these things become commodities and exchangeable. In this way, the work of the X-ray tech is made interchangeable with the work of the construction worker, not as the creation of a specific useful thing, but as a process of value creation.

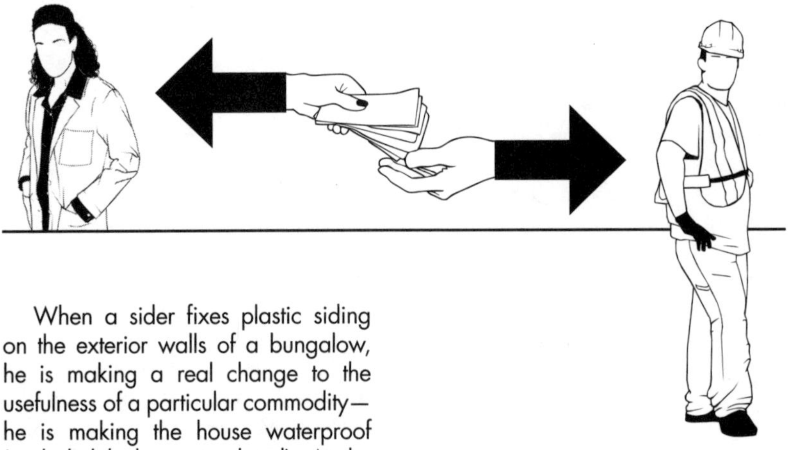

When a sider fixes plastic siding on the exterior walls of a bungalow, he is making a real change to the usefulness of a particular commodity—he is making the house waterproof (and slightly better insulated). At the same time he is adding value to the commodity—his work takes part in forming an average for the amount of work necessary to put siding on a bungalow in a particular society. It doesn't matter how much time and effort he puts into putting up the siding on this or that particular house. His work adds value to the house based on a socially necessary average amount of work time the task should take. If, next year, a new, faster method for fixing plastic siding to houses becomes widespread, the value of all houses with plastic siding will fall, whether or not they were made using that method.

There is constant exchange of different kinds of commodities.

Things appear to have value because of the social relations between people producing different useful things. Value exists when, in order for useful things to get from the people who make them to the people who need them, they have to pass through the intermediate step of being bought and sold (or bartered or otherwise exchanged).

When the buyer looks at a house, he sees what it can be used for—a

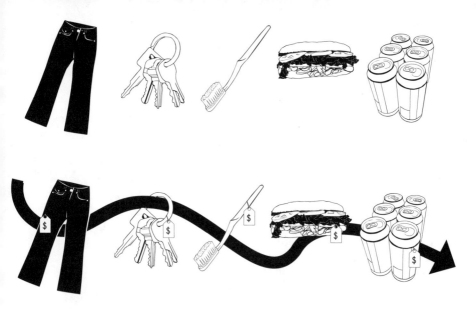

warm place to sleep, to make food, to have a party. For the seller, the house is a blob of value waiting to be turned into money. He doesn't care about the heated pool and the outdoor barbecue, except as a hook to get someone to buy the house. Like any commodity seller, he's in it for the money.

But simply buying and selling houses at their value doesn't make money. It just means that the value stored up in a house is turned into value stored up in money, which could then be traded for other commodities. But the owner of a construction company is not just a commodity seller. He's a capitalist.

In a capitalist society everyone's activity is interchangeable and we are all equal as people with commodities for sale. At the same time most of us have nothing to sell but our ability to work. Everything that is necessary to make useful things is owned and controlled by a class of capitalists—it is their private property.

X-ray techs can't take X-rays without access to expensive X-ray machines in the hospital, owned by the hospital's shareholders. Cement

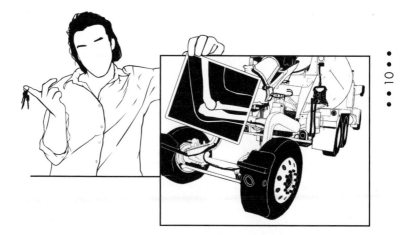

masons can't lay the foundations for houses without access to expensive concrete mixing trucks. Those of us who don't have property we can make money from are forced to sell our ability to work to a capitalist—we become wage workers.

Our ability to work is like any other commodity in that its value is based on the value of all the things that go into making it. We have to be paid enough to pay for all the food, clothes, rent, phone service, education and training, healthcare, gasoline, liquor, and sleeping pills we need to keep showing up every morning able to work. Our ability to work is not like other commodities in that it creates new value.

A box of nails and a pile of two-by-fours come into a construction site with a value based on the amount of work necessary to make them and transport them to the site. They are the combined product of workers in a nail factory, a saw mill, a paper mill, miners, loggers, truckers, guys driving forklifts in warehouses, and hundreds of other workers. The work of all these people is stored up in the box of nails and pile of two-by-fours as value. They are labor already turned into things—dead labor.

As the wood and nails are used up and made into an interior wall of a house, they transfer their value to the house. The value of the nail gun used to drive the nails transfers its value slowly to all the different walls on which it is used based on the average lifetime of nail guns. But an interior wall is worth more than a pile of wood and nails, and some wear and tear on a nail gun. The difference is the work the framer did building the wall.

Our ability to work is not used up like a raw material or a machine, transferring its value directly to the product. Our living labor creates enough value to replace our wages and more. We're paid a wage and expected to work for a specific

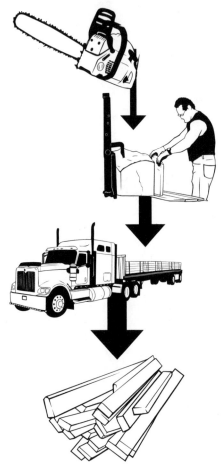

amount of time. As we build a wall we use up bits of dead labor. We both transfer their value to the wall and at the same time add more value by doing work. Whether our wages are calculated hourly, daily, weekly, or monthly, our living labor adds more value to the houses we build during that time than we are paid in wages. This surplus value belongs to the boss.

A house is an expensive thing, so usually a capitalist with his money invested in house production has a contract with a buyer before he breaks ground. Say, for example, he gets a contract to build a mansion

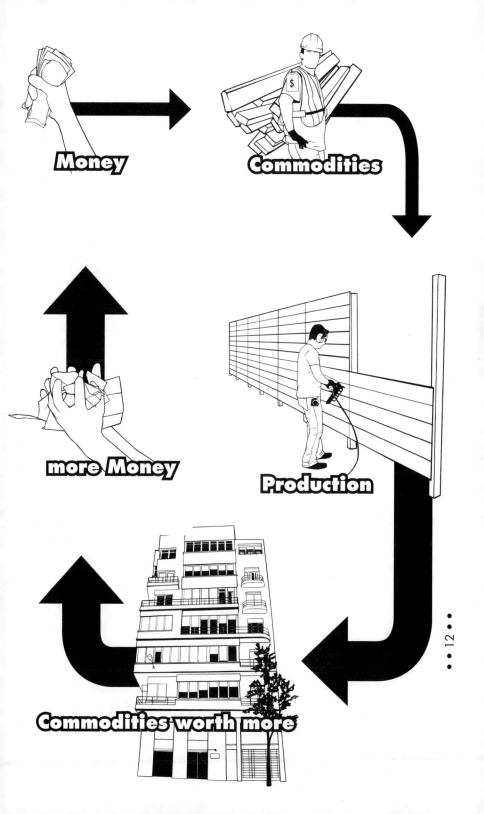

Money

Commodities

more Money

Production

Commodities worth more

by the beach. He starts with money. Then he buys the commodities he needs to make the house. These are raw materials (like nails, wood, drywall, cement, pipes, copper wire) and machines and tools (like drills, ladders, strings of temporary lighting, scaffolding, forklifts). And he hires an appropriate mix of construction workers. These are all brought together at the construction site and set in motion making the beach-side mansion. When finished, the product is a commodity worth more than the means of production and wages. He is then paid for the job and his capital is freed up to start again. This time he has a bit more, and can maybe take on a bigger contract.

In reality, a construction site is more often a bunch of overlapping production processes. One capitalist has the contract to build the house (or houses) and acts as a general contractor. He hires some of the workers who will spend the most time on the construction site (such as the framers, the laborers, and maybe a few operating engineers to run the big machinery). The electrical systems, the plumbing, the HVAC, the roofing and siding, the insulation and drywall, the painting, the finish carpentry, the tile and concrete work he leaves to specialized subcontractors. As far as the production process he's involved

in is concerned, the products of the various subcontractors enter as raw materials to be built into the house, even if they have not been put together yet. The capital of the subcontractor moves in the same circuit.

Say a finish carpentry company gets the contract to install all the cabinets and decorative windowsills and door frames in the mansion. The owner of the company starts with money. Then he buys the required raw materials, tools, and machines (finished wood, plastic fasteners, glue, step ladders, nails, nail guns, etc.), hires the required workers and puts them to work installing the cabinets and door and window frames. These are a commodity, which is sold to the general contractor. The money is more than his initial investment and can be reinvested to expand the company. The value of the business expands. Whether the finished commodity is a house or a part of a house (or even repairs or remodeling of a house) the process of capital accumulation is the same. By getting his money to flow through a production process in which surplus value is created, the capitalist makes more money—his capital expands.

But the owner of a construction company doesn't make any distinction between money invested in living and dead labor. His profit is surplus value, but it doesn't look like surplus value. The fact that his profit comes from paying workers less than the value they create at work is hidden in the normal business of buying and selling commodities. He spends his money on everything needed to run his business, and when the job's done, he gets a return. The difference is his profit. By comparing his profit to the total capital he invested, he gets a rate of profit for a specific period of time.

Say an HVAC contractor spends $100,000 over the course of a year

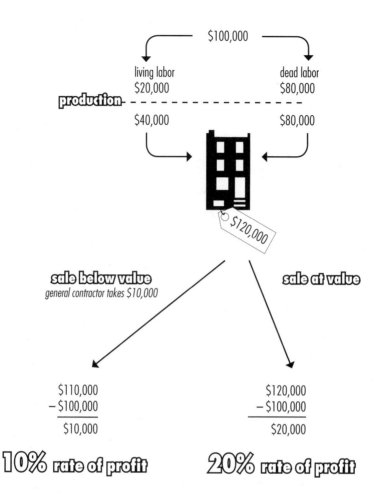

$100,000

living labor
$20,000

dead labor
$80,000

production

$40,000

$80,000

$120,000

sale below value
general contractor takes $10,000

sale at value

$110,000
−$100,000
―――――――
$10,000

$120,000
−$100,000
―――――――
$20,000

10% rate of profit

20% rate of profit

installing the heating, ventilation, and air conditioning systems in a residential high-rise. Say $80,000 of it was used to buy dead labor (fans, heaters and air conditioners of various sizes, sheets of galvanized steel, duct tape and insulation, saws, tin snips, extension cords, replacements for the wear and tear on the company van, etc.) and $20,000 to buy living labor (wages).

Say the employees took half their time at work to add enough value to the HVAC systems they were assembling to pay their wages, and the rest of the time they added surplus

value. This would mean that the value of the HVAC system was $120,000. If the contractor was paid $120,000 he would have an annual rate of profit of 20%—quite good. If the general contractor only paid him $110,000, he would still make an annual profit of 10%, but the surplus value created by his employees would be divided equally between him and the general contractor.

But there's never only one contractor. Each separate enterprise in the same line of business competes against the others on the open market. Buyers won't buy a product that doesn't work right, and they'll

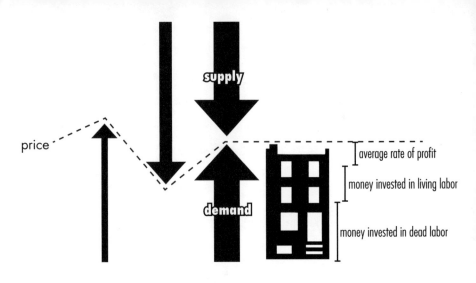

price

average rate of profit

money invested in living labor

money invested in dead labor

buy the cheapest one of the same quality. In this way a market price is formed for installing all the HVAC systems in a residential high-rise.

This price can be pushed up if there are a lot of buildings to outfit and not that many HVAC contractors in the area, or it can be pushed down if a lot of contractors are competing for the contracts on a few buildings. When the price drops it just means that more of the surplus value is going to the general contractor. When it rises, the HVAC contractor is keeping more of it. The prices are constantly being pushed up and down based on market conditions, but supply and demand cannot explain the price. At the point where supply and demand are equal, they don't explain anything.

The price of an installed HVAC system (like any commodity) moves around an equilibrium price. That equilibrium price is the value of the

capital invested in the dead labor plus that invested in living labor plus an average rate of profit for the industry. Contractors making significantly less than the average rate of profit will go out of business, and their contracts will go to those who are making more. This competition makes the different enterprises producing a similar product compare and copy each other's internal organization and work processes. If one contractor starts using a new material to make ducts out of that is cheaper than galvanized steel, he will lower his costs, make more profit than the average, and be able to sell his commodities cheaper. All the other contractors will have to start using the new material or go out of business. As they make the switch, his competitive advantage will disappear.

But it's not just capital invested in the same industry that competes.

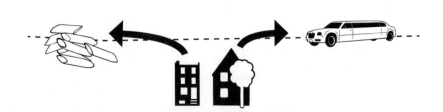

From the point of view of value trying to expand itself, any business is as good as the next. All that matters is the rate of profit. If a decent-sized HVAC contractor sees that limousine companies or pasta manufacturers are making more profit for the same investment, he can sell his company and buy a fleet of limousines or a pasta factory. As more and more capital that was in the business of installing ventilation systems moves into the business of taxiing around celebrities and taking high school kids to the prom, the price of limousine service will fall and the price of HVAC systems will rise. An average rate of profit is formed—weighted for how much capital is invested in different businesses.

Competition means that each individual enterprise does not keep the surplus value it squeezed out of its workers, but will tend to make profit based on the average rate of profit in the market it operates in. If specific sectors continue to produce at a below average rate of profit, firms or even whole industries will see their investment evaporate and go out of business.

In reality there are all sorts of barriers to the movement of capital,

and profit rates are never fully equalized. If one company owns all the lumber processing plants in the area, it can drive up the price of two-by-fours. It would then have a higher rate of profit because when construction companies paid its inflated prices it would be capturing some of the surplus value created by their workers. Its domination of the entire market would be a barrier to the equalization of the rate of profit.

But monopolies are only the most extreme example of barriers to the movement of capital. Take a contractor who has been running the same plumbing company for 40 years and employs a couple of his nephews. He knows that he could make a higher rate of profit if he sold it and invested his money in an upscale bar catering to yuppies in a gay neighborhood, but he doesn't. His prejudice against homosexuals, or his religious conviction against the consumption of alcohol, or just his attachment to the family business is a barrier to the movement of his capital.

Whether they're monopolies, trade tariffs, different tax structures, religious beliefs, different health and safety laws, or just individual

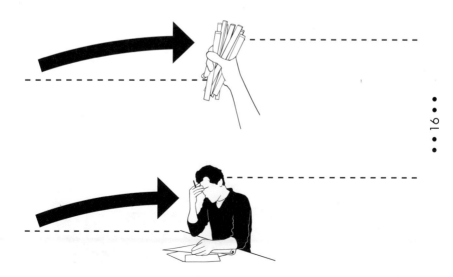

attachments to a particular line of work or a particular neighborhood, the various barriers to the movement of capital don't stop the market from functioning. They form the contours of the market.

Still, the wider the difference between the rates of profit the barriers are keeping apart, the more pressure that is put on those barriers. The constant movement of capital back and forth between industries and regions tends to have a corrosive effect on anything that stands in the way of equalizing the rate of profit.

All this competition puts a lot of pressure on the owner of a construction company. His company has got to not just make a profit but a competitive profit. He's got to grow or die. It's not easy being a capitalist.

He's always worried about his profit rate. He's always worried about whether his employees are wasting raw materials or whether we're working hard enough or whether we're abusing his machines and creating more than an average amount of wear and tear. If he wants to remain a business owner, he's got to push us to work harder, faster, longer, and for less money—he's got to be an asshole.

Every day at work at the construction site is a constant battle, as the boss tries to squeeze as much surplus value out of us as possible. When he can get us to start work a little earlier, leave a little later, or work a little harder and faster, he is raising the profit rate at our expense. When we take smoke breaks when we're supposed to be working, when we throw away usable parts rather than walk down several floors to put them back by the gang box, when we steal tools or take extra-long lunches, we're making our lives a little easier and at the same time cutting into the profit rate.

We don't care about the company. Our interests are directly opposed to the boss's and to the whole process of capital accumulation in general.

We have to sell our ability to work in order to buy the things we need to survive. The fact that some guys will bring in some homemade burritos to sell at lunch, or will sell some drugs on the side, or will steal copper pipes and wire from the site to sell for scrap, doesn't change the fact that we are dependent on selling our ability to work to a boss—dependent on a wage. Our time spent at work is not our own—it's that part of our lives that we just want to be over.

In order to make a living we're forced to give over a huge portion of our lives to the boss. We make jokes

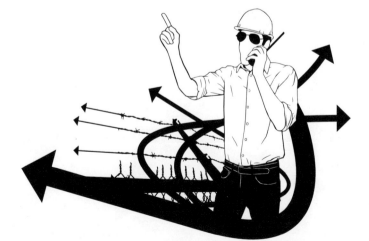

comparing work to prison. A new guy on a job will be asked, "How much time have you done?" Older guys who've been in the trades for years are called "lifers." The guy who has given notice and is quitting next week is a "short-timer." We complain about our boss and say we're going to quit and go work at a real company that treats its employees right. There's always stories about "the good boss" or "the good company to work for," but somehow it's never our current one. Attitudes to the boss usually range from guarded indifference to white-hot hatred, depending on who he picks on and how much he tries to push us around.

Every day we can see our activity being turned into things, as buildings rise out of the ground and are filled with wires, pipes, and ducts. But in the houses we build, we don't see protection from the weather and privacy. We see a big meaningless object that we're forced to work on and someone else makes money from.

Single-family suburban bungalows, dark basement apartments, reinforced concrete housing towers, trailers, and beach-side mansions are not just dead labor. They're capital. They're dead labor that needs to move and expand by squeezing living labor. Houses as well as vans full of parts and tools, sheets of steel, rolls of copper wire, backhoes, and cement mixing trucks appear as capital only because of the relations between the people making them. They are owned and controlled by capitalists and worked on by wage workers without property we can make money from. The representative of dead labor controls living labor and forces us to work so that dead labor can expand. This class relationship shapes everything else in a capitalist society.

Socialization, Separation, and Subcontracting

*"The secret of managing is
to keep the guys who hate you
away from the guys who are undecided."*

Casey Stengel

A construction site is the shared workplace of workers with lots of different bosses. At many construction sites, people working for a small family business work side by side with people working for a large subcontractor. Workers hired by the boss directly or through a union hiring hall coordinate their work with workers hired through a temp agency. Workers with and without legal working papers work next to each other but for different companies.

The various tasks required to put a building together are divided up and made the specialized work of different trades. At a typical construction site, where a luxury condominium high-rise tower is being built, there will be operating engineers to run the dump trucks, backhoes, bulldozers, forklifts, and cranes, iron workers to put together the steel skeleton of the building, framers to put in the structural wood and light metal such as the interior walls and drop ceilings, cement masons to tie together the rebar and pour concrete for the building's foundation, sidewalks, patios, and the walls and ceilings of the underground parking garage. There will be electricians to install the electrical systems, HVAC guys to install the heating, ventilation, and air conditioning systems, plumbers to

install the systems that bring in clean water, take out waste water and the sprinklers. There will be laborers to unload and distribute materials around the site, to run the more physically demanding machines like jackhammers and tampers, to direct traffic when the work requires tearing up parts of the roads around the job site and generally to do odd jobs for the general contractor. There will be laborers hired from a temp agency who come in every couple of days to remove garbage from the site. There will be insulators, drywallers, finish carpenters, elevator installers, window and door installers, garage door installers, roofers and siders, stone masons, floor guys, carpet guys, tile guys. There will be specialized workers to install the carbon monoxide detection system in the parking garage, and others to install the security alarms and cameras.

There will be landscapers to put in the shrubbery and the rows of palm trees lining the building's entrance. Finally there will be cleaners to come in and make the place look nice before prospective condo buyers come and look at it. Some of these workers will be hired by the general contractor directly, but most of them will work for subcontracting companies.

The different trades all require different materials and machines, some of which are very expensive. By having specialized subcontractors, costs are lowered and the amount of time that capital is sitting around not making money is reduced. A roofing company doesn't need to buy expensive machinery for making precision cuts to granite countertops, and a tile company doesn't need to buy scaffolding and safety harnesses that allow people to work on the roofs and sides of buildings. Some of the trades (like the framers or laborers) can spend a year or more on the same construction site, while others (like garage door or security system installers) will be on the site for only a couple of days. This means that it would be necessary to mass-produce houses on a huge scale before it would be cost-effective for

one company to hire all the different building workers.

By subcontracting, the general contractor doesn't need to keep elevator installers, who can't work until the building's skeleton is all together, on the payroll. And elevator installing contractors can line up a bunch of jobs one after another, keep their workers working, and keep their tools from sitting around rusting. Sometimes it even makes business sense for subcontractors to further subcontract out parts of their responsibility. An electrical subcontractor will get a specialized subcontractor to install just the low-voltage electrical systems, a plumbing company will subcontract out just for the sprinkler system.

Subcontracting also distributes risk. Since houses are rarely built from a standardized model, there are all sorts of things that have to be figured out during construction on each specific site. This means that there are all sorts of things that can go wrong and slow down the production of any given building. Disruptions that slow down the work of one trade can easily slow down all the others. If one company did all the work on a particular building, it would take on

all the risk. Most subcontractors run several job sites at once, however. They'll be involved in building some condominiums, a mansion, a block of apartments, an old folks' home, and a school all at the same time. This means that problems at one job can't cascade into their other jobs. The risk is distributed more evenly across all the capital invested in house production.

Some very small contractors are only able to take on one job at a time. This means that the boss is usually there all the time supervising his employees. Any contractor large enough to run a couple jobs at once, will need foremen. The owner of the company will make bids, buy new equipment, hire and fire people, deal with the general contractor, and travel around to check on the progress of each job. The daily management of each site will be done by a foreman. The foreman is often the only representative of management on site, and it's his job to make us work hard. If he doesn't, he will get fired. Still, the company's profit is not his profit, so he is a less enthusiastic enforcer than the boss. He can kick us off his job site for not working hard, but often he can't fire

us. Usually the foreman will be an older worker who's been in the trades for a long time and is expected to divide his time between working on the building and supervising other employees. Sometimes foremen are union members. Whether we respect or hate the foreman depends mostly on how much he acts as an enforcer for the boss—how much he does his job.

Subcontracting means that the workers in the same company are separated from each other, distributed across a number of job sites. At the same time each construction site has a unified chain of command, and starts to look a bit like an individual company. The general contractor runs the job. He sets work rules for the site and can kick workers he hasn't hired off the site for breaking them. He, or a supervisor he's hired, coordinates all the work with the foremen of the different trades, who then pass orders down to the workers. The bosses of the different subcontracting companies are only brought in to talk about money or when there's a problem or if the supervisor wants to put extra pressure on the foreman to get his guys working faster. This means that the general contractor

acts like a boss, even to workers he hasn't hired directly. Attitudes to the general contractor or his supervisors tend to be similar to attitudes toward the boss. And we fight against the general contractor as well as our own boss as they work together to try to squeeze more out of us.

The work process itself makes us work together in groups and coordinate the work with the other trades. Drywallers take on different tasks and work together in teams to put up the drywall more quickly. The drywallers have to talk to the electricians and plumbers to know whether or not a wire or pipe is supposed to stick out of the wall, or be buried in the wall. The groups of electricians and plumbers need to talk to each other and to the tile guys and finish carpenters to figure out how sinks, outlets and tiling, countertops and cabinets fit together.

We work with the same people a lot and get to know them pretty well. Conversations that start about how to do the work quickly become about the football game last weekend, about our wives, girlfriends, and kids, about this one crazy iron worker someone knew, and then about how shitty the work is or how the boss is an asshole. The work is monotonous, and socializing usually means joking around, stapling someone's tools to the floor, locking someone in the porta-potty, throwing screws out the window at the guys directing traffic. We give each other strange nicknames and draw on each other's hard hats. We take smoke breaks together and go out for drinks after work. We stop being isolated individuals and form groups of workers who trust each other, work together, and can act together.

The biggest obstacle to forming these groups is the division of labor

itself. Workers doing more skilled work will think they're better than the apprentices and workers doing less skilled work and order them around. Newer employees will assume that the workers who have been there a while are friends with the boss. When we're all being pushed to do more, faster, it's easy to cut corners in a way that fucks over the other trades. Drywallers will bury electrical boxes meant for lights and outlets rather than take the time to cut holes. Electricians will leave a pile of garbage in a room that gets in the plumber's way. A plumber will smash big holes in the drywall looking for a sprinkler head that was buried. This is a constant source of friction and can lead to arguments and even occasional fistfights.

This conflict is made worse because the division of labor is overlaid with cultural differences. The workers doing the less skilled, more physical work are often immigrants who don't speak the language. Often the only one who knows both languages well is the foreman. This division is institutionalized by subcontracting, as each company will hire workers from similar backgrounds. The workers in a company form a kind of ethnic community. This means that when workers from different trades are stepping on each other's toes, it's only a small step from "Those stupid drywallers..." to "Those stupid Mexicans..." or from "Those lazy siders..." to "Those lazy Polacks..."

And workers who are racist against each other don't socialize together and have a very difficult time organizing together against the boss. Unless these divisions lead to fights that actually slow down the work process, they are a good thing from the point of view of the boss.

Still, even a racist can feel the surplus value constantly being pumped out of him. At the same time we're assembling a building that will make the boss a lot of money, we're finishing off each paycheck just about the time the next one comes. Even the boss's brother-in-law, who's a snitch, will try to get out of hard work if he can. Even the extreme right-winger who hates it when the government interferes with the rights of private property will steal from work. Even the guy who complains about the "lazy immigrants" slacks off on the job when he can get away with it. Our hostility to the work doesn't come from our political ideas. It comes from the fact that we are being exploited as wage workers. We have interests that are directly opposed to the company's interests. Still, the less internally conflicted we can become, the better we can get at fighting the boss. We can consciously plan and coordinate our resistance. We can see who our real allies and enemies are likely to be.

A company's internal structure and work process create patterns of socialization and separation. These are the terrain on which we fight with management, but they are also a weapon in the hands of the boss. We are brought together and divided up in order to pump as much surplus value out of us as possible. But when we work together, we begin to see that we have similar interests—interests that are directly opposed to our bosses' interests. As we form groups that slack off, steal from work and cover for each other, we cut into the rate of profit, and the boss has to respond. He can respond by changing around work patterns. He may supervise us directly, or hire more workers, so the foreman can spend more time making sure we're working hard. Like most decisions the boss makes, though, this will be made on a cost-benefit analysis, and constant supervision is expensive. Instead, he may separate workers he thinks are causing problems. He will have us work in different parts of the building or move us around to different construction sites. This can break up work groups and cut down on resistance. It can also mean that a culture of resistance spreads throughout the company.

Alternately, he may try to neutralize our informal work groups by joining them or getting someone he trusts to join them. He'll come work with us for a few hours, or take us out to lunch one day. Usually we'll be friendly enough while he's there and then go back to slacking off once he's gone. More often, he'll send in a different worker he trusts to work with us. Since we're almost always doing less than we're supposed to, this will mean we have to work harder until we can be sure the new worker isn't a snitch. If he's not a bad guy, he will soon become part of the work group. If he acts like a little boss and tries to get us to work harder, he will be treated like one. He'll get a nickname like "office bitch" or "ass face" and no one will help him with any tasks unless the boss is standing there watching. People won't talk to him and his work will be made miserable until he asks to work by himself or with someone else. We know how to use socialization and separation as well.

Standing up for each other, forming groups, corrupting workers who sympathize with the boss, and exposing and excluding snitches— these are what the everyday struggle at a construction site is made of. When it's going well, it can make our lives a lot less miserable. It is the foundation for any larger fight against management.

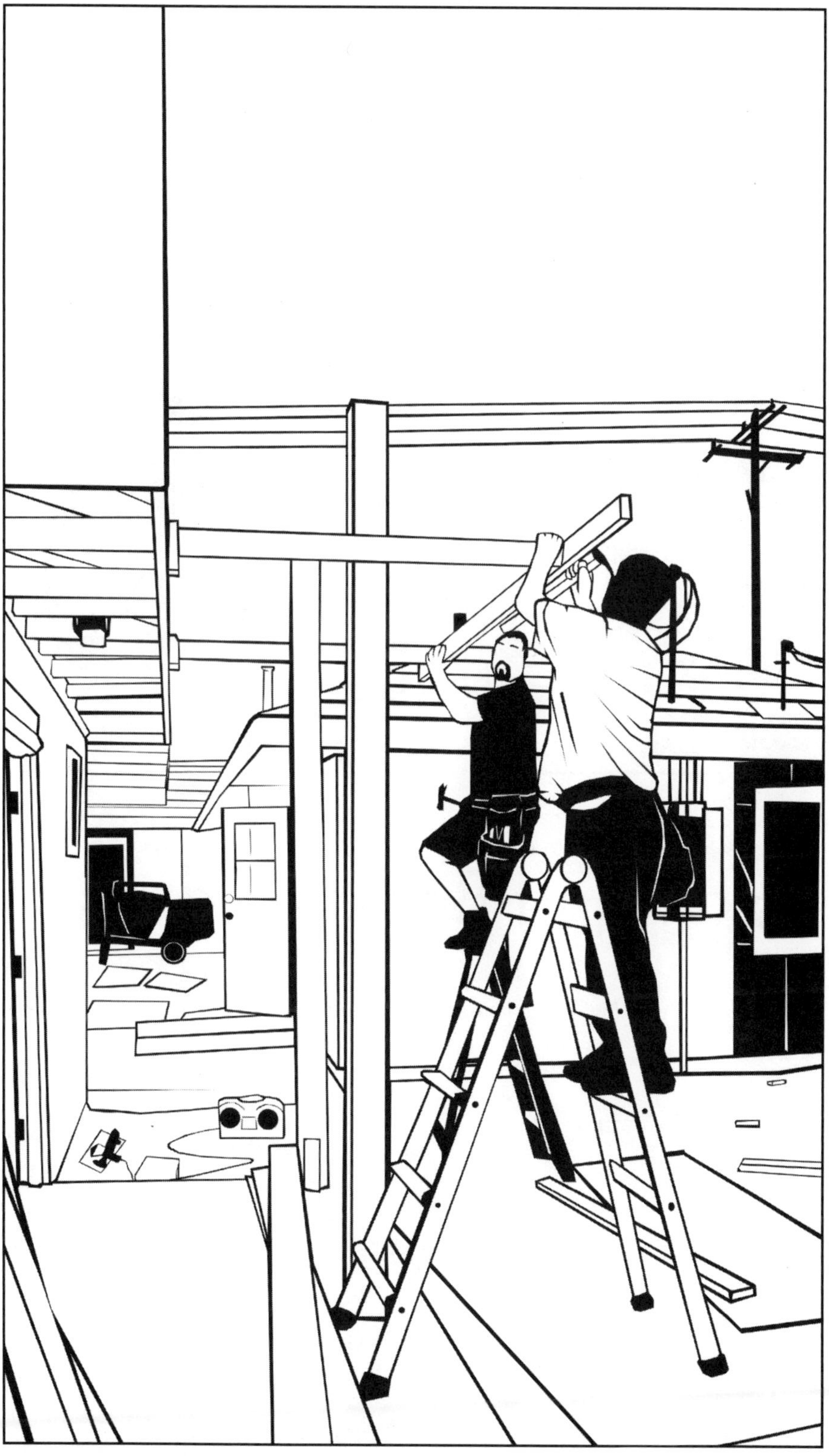

Skill and Backwardness

"I will make houses like they make cars."

Le Corbusier

Houses are not just built for a profit. The work process used to make them is constantly under pressure to change to make as much profit as possible.

Individual jobs are broken up into small tasks that can be repeated quickly. In a team of drywallers, one will measure the areas to be covered and screw the sheets to the wall, another will cut sheets to fit, another will come along after and spread tape and spackle over the joints where pieces of drywall fit together, and a fourth will smooth out the mud with a taping knife. When

Plastic snap-in connectors replace steel screw-in connectors. The roller or the paint-spraying machine replace the paintbrush. The nail gun replaces the hammer and the sawsall replaces the saw. These are all expensive, but they allow the painter, the electrician, or the carpenter to do more work in the same amount of time. When a company first introduces a new machine it can make a lot more profit because it is producing much more efficiently than the industry average. As a new machine becomes widespread, producing with that machine becomes the new industry

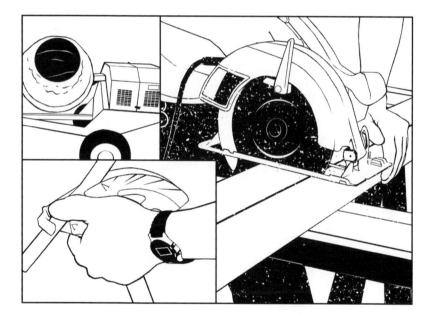

jobs are chopped up like this, we get very good at doing our individual task and can do it quickly and efficiently. At the same time, the work gets repetitive and boring.

The machines, tools, parts, and materials we work with are designed and redesigned to speed up the work process, or to allow us to do the same work cheaper. The reusable wire nuts that electricians use to connect wires in a light fixture are replaced with quicker push-in connectors built into the light fixture.

average. The labor of the painter is spread out over more walls in a given period of time, and the value of a painted wall drops. A painting contractor has to invest a higher proportion of his money in dead labor (such as paint-spraying machines) as compared to living labor.

As tasks are divided up between a number of employees, and more and more machines are introduced, jobs tend to become simpler, more repetitive, less skilled. Skilled tradesmen tend to become more

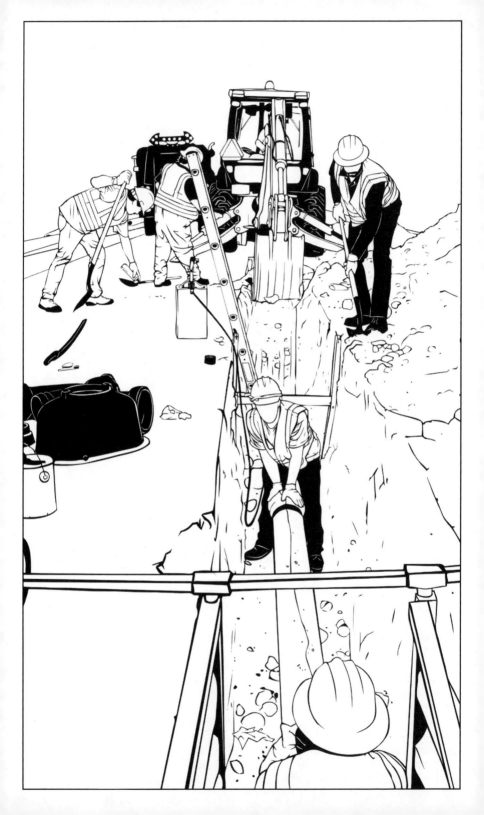

like installers and installers tend to become more like factory workers. As jobs become less skilled, employees need less training (and therefore tend to get paid less and are easier to replace).

after putting the pipes in a few, the plumbers will get the hang of it and be able to go much faster. Still, all the apartment buildings on a block are not the same, and all the blocks in a city are definitely different.

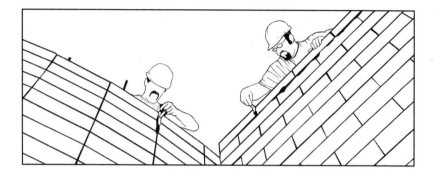

Still, the carpenter's laser level is nothing compared to the laser checkout scanner used by a cashier. In many ways, the construction industry is very backward. New technology hasn't been able to reshape the whole work process around it. The only areas of construction that have really been mechanized are excavation and lifting materials—and not even these on some small sites. New machines on a construction site are usually just high-tech tools. They tend to feel more like an extension of our body than something that imposes a mechanical rhythm on our work. Construction materials can be high-tech, but construction is not. The workers adding fiber-optic cables, motion sensors, and solar panels to a house are often using nothing more than hand tools, a cordless drill, and a ladder.

In order for new technology and the division of labor to really increase productivity, houses would have to be mass-produced—house production would have to take place on a large scale, and house design would have to be standardized. This has had only very limited success. The units in an apartment building can be designed exactly the same, so

Trailers and doublewides are made from standardized designs in factory-like conditions and transported to the buyer. But most homes aren't transportable, and designs are different for different locations. Houses have to be built on land somewhere. In order to mass-produce a neighborhood, a developer has to buy up all the land first. This means coaxing or coercing all the different owners of the land he wants to build on to sell to him.

Even when they can get their hands on large areas of land, developers often build in small chunks. Houses are extremely durable. Unlike restaurants, or even car manufacturers, the house-building industry can't rely on replacing old houses as a steady source of demand. The building industry tends to boom when the economy as a whole is growing and to crash when the growth stops. Making an apartment building can take a long time, and the market can change quickly during that time. This creates an extra incentive to build quickly—which means building small. A company building an L-shaped apartment building will sometimes build one wing and

make sure it is sold before building the other half. A large company will build a number of small sites, rather than one large one. This (as well as the relatively cheap costs of getting into the construction business) means that there are often lots of small contractors competing right alongside the big ones.

The backwardness of the construction industry is a bad thing from the point of view of productivity, not necessarily for us. The fact that there are rarely standardized designs means that individual workers have to figure out how things fit together, and we often have a lot of room to do things however we think makes the most sense. The architects are never right the first time. The plans for the HVAC system, the windows, the plumbing, and the framing will often not work together. After a few jokes at the expense of the architectural profession, we'll have to work with the guys from the other trades to figure out how to make things work. We get an idea of how the whole building has to fit together. We have to think a bit on top of just doing physical labor. The limited use of machines and the fact that building often goes on at a bunch of scattered, small sites, means that each worker has to learn how to do a number of different tasks. A job from start to finish can take months, and at each stage we might be doing different things. The backwardness of the work process means that the work

requires a variety of skills and quite a bit of decision-making on our part. In this, the job of a skilled construction worker is closer to that of a white-collar worker like a teacher than it is to the job of an auto worker. Keeping in mind how a building has to fit together as a whole, and using a bit of thought and skill at work, makes the job a bit less boring. It doesn't change the fact that we're doing all this to make money for the boss. And once capital can make houses (or teach) like it makes cars, it will.

Unlike more specialist white-collar jobs, we have to learn almost all of our skills on the job. Formal apprenticeships often require some classroom time, but this is usually quite small compared to the amount of time spent learning while working. This means that on any construction site, in any trade, workers with lots of experience work side by side with fresh apprentices. Skill and experience are very important in how we relate to each other. The first question a new worker on a job site will usually ask his coworkers is "How long have you been in the trade?" and he will quickly figure who he has more experience than and who less. Experience in some trades is officially recognized by "cards." By working a number of hours, passing a course or a test, skilled tradesmen are legally recognized as journeymen. This usually means more pay and more authority on the job site. In other trades, the skill of different workers and their differing wages are just judged by the boss.

The boss has to place a lot of trust in his skilled workers. The speed and quality of the work depends on lots of individual decisions about how to use hand tools and how to accomplish tasks. We often work with very little supervision. The boss or the foreman will give us something to do and then check later that what we put together works. In some companies skilled workers will work on job sites all by themselves. We often are expected to buy our own tools and can choose which ones to buy. The boss of a medium-size subcontracting company is an outsider and usually doesn't really know what's going on at each of his jobs. He profits from our work and puts pressure on us to do more and faster, but he usually gives us a lot of room to organize it however we want. We like this freedom and are very annoyed when it is attacked. The quickest way for the boss to get his workers to hate him is to force them to work in specific ways.

This control over the work can create a kind of professionalism among certain skilled construction workers. There are a lot of real skills we learn, and we can tell which of our coworkers actually know what they're doing. We take a certain pride in being able to do complicated skilled work. We like to use our skills when we can to fix something at home or to help a friend build an addition onto their house. This craft pride is the main way that management appeals to skilled workers. There is an attempt to create a kind of community around "the trade." The community includes the boss, the foreman, and the skilled journeymen, but not the apprentices who are just learning the trade (and definitely not the workers doing less skilled jobs, like the laborers, landscapers, cleaners, etc.). On this basis, the work is seen as just

something that needs to be done, and skilled workers are supposed to help enforce it on the less skilled.

Tasks are further divided up within the workers. The shittiest work is reserved for the workers newest to the trade. An apprentice might spend his entire first year in the electrical or plumbing trades, digging ditches, carrying heavy materials around the site, sweeping up, and organizing parts and materials. An experienced electrician might spend almost all his time doing electrical panels, and might take it as an insult if it is suggested that he should help pull wires—let alone help sweep up. Skilled workers will sometimes act like little bosses, ordering around their apprentices, and refusing to do anything but "gravy work." This is particularly bad when skill and experience don't overlap. As an apprentice, there's nothing worse than doing the shit work for a journeyman who doesn't know what he's doing. All the mistakes somehow magically become your fault, even if you were only sweeping the floor and unloading materials all day.

The separation of work into "journeyman tasks" and "apprentice tasks" is made worse by the fact that a lot of skill is simply made up. A journeyman who had to do shit work for years before he was taught the trade, will think it's unfair when

apprentices get to do tasks that are "above their skill level." He will artificially inflate the division between journeyman tasks and apprentice tasks—and the apprentices he's working with will hate his guts. True, an apprentice on his first day can't be expected to know how to wire up a building. Still, there's no reason why you should have a year of experience sweeping before you can learn how to pull wires, or that it should take a year of pulling wires before you're ready to do electrical panels. These divisions are not based on the real skill curve. They don't even really help speed up the work process.

These differences are mainly there to get skilled workers to take on the boss's perspective. Journeymen always have to do some supervision of apprentices to make sure they know what they're doing (and apprentices usually appreciate a journeyman who will take the time to explain things and answer questions). A skilled worker who acts like a little boss is something entirely different. He's a cost-saving measure. From the boss's perspective, a journeyman who will work at the same time as making sure the apprentices aren't slacking off is the cheapest kind of supervision available—much cheaper than hiring a full-time, supervisory foreman. Also, since the more skilled workers usually set the tone for the culture of work on a job site, a skilled worker with a strong sense of professionalism can make sure that the work groups that do form are harmless to the boss.

This identification with the work is real, based in the loose supervision and the freedom that skilled workers have to self-manage the work. It is also very limited. It begins to crack when it becomes clear that experience and authority in a company are not the same thing. The guy who's got two years of experience gets a company

truck, while the guy who's got ten doesn't. The boss's brother-in-law gets to run a site himself, while a more skilled journeymen is passed over. A construction company isn't an institution for building houses and teaching people the skills to build houses. It is an institution for squeezing surplus value out of workers—workers who get nothing but a wage out of it and need to be kept under control. Building houses and learning skills are quite secondary. The boss gives authority to the workers who he trusts to keep the other ones under control. The boss needs to keep all his employees (apprentices and journeymen) working as hard as possible for as little money as possible. Professionalism loses some of its allure when the foreman asks us, one professional to another, to work on the weekend so he can get a job done on time. It loses even more when the boss yells at us to work faster or he's going to lose money and have to fire us.

Differences in skill and experience can divide up the workers and get us fighting each other. It can also just be the background to the work and joking around at work. We'll make fun of the old man who's been in the trade for years who randomly gives his opinion on all sorts of things, whether they're related to the work or not. The baby-shit green apprentice will be told to go get "a box of ohms," a "left-handed pole stretcher," or some other nonexistent tool from the general contractor. After a few jokes like this he'll get the hang of the work culture, and learn the specialized vocabulary necessary to communicate on a construction site.

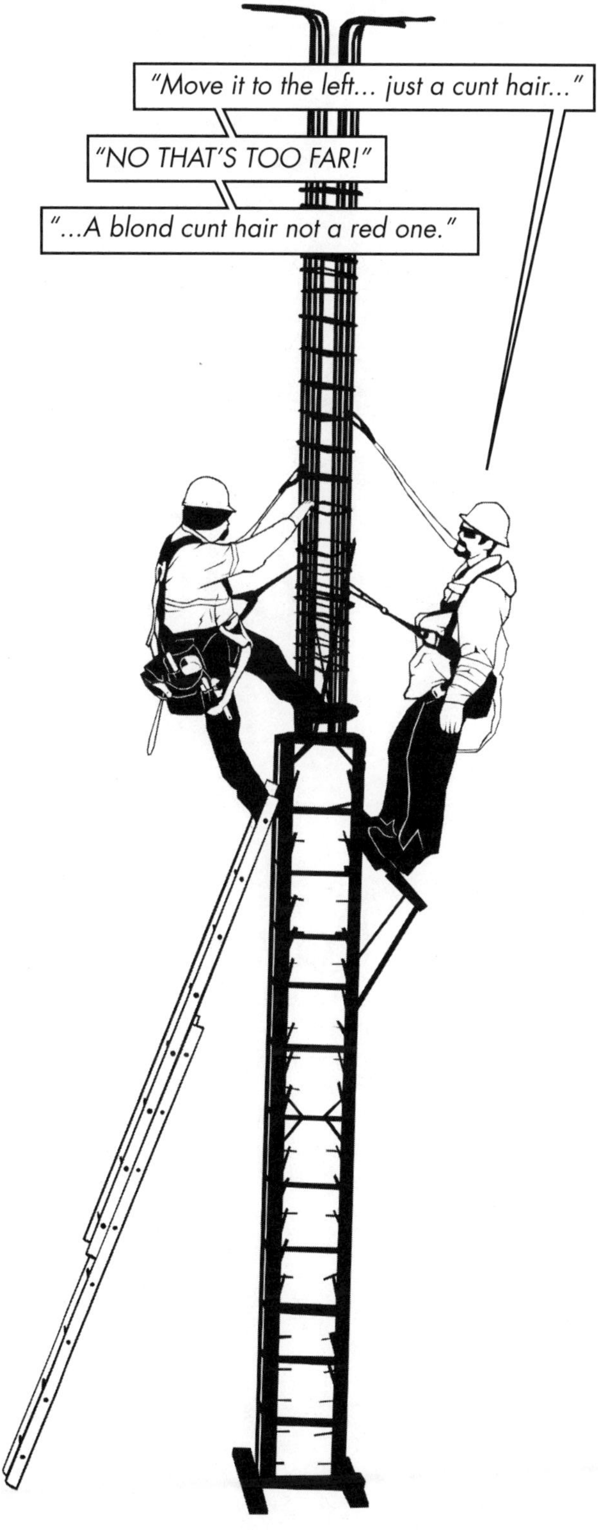
"Move it to the left... just a cunt hair..."
"NO THAT'S TOO FAR!"
"...A blond cunt hair not a red one."

The Pace of Work

*"Accomplishing the impossible means only
the boss will add it to your regular duties."*

Doug Larson

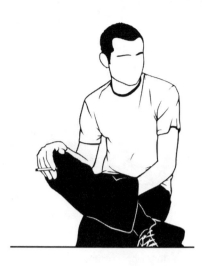

There is no "automatic" pace of work on a construction site. There is no assembly line for the boss to speed up and no customers to come in all at once at dinner time. With the exception of drying concrete, the materials and machines we work with do not impose a rhythm on the work. We have a lot of room to start and stop working whenever we want. The work process is porous. Carrying around materials, hammering, setting up scaffolding, and untangling extension cords, are interspersed with standing around smoking, telling jokes, and spacing out while we wait for someone to set up scaffolding or untangle some electrical cord spaghetti.

The boss needs to keep us working as hard as possible and get the most out of us he can. In a small company where we work with the boss, this can mean that he's there personally yelling at us to "hurry the fuck up!" In a larger company this is the job of the foreman.

Since we're usually making very visible changes to the building, the supervision doesn't need to be this tight. The foreman can just stop by and see how much we've gotten done and the boss of a subcontracting company can come to the job site once every week or two to check up on his foremen.

This loose supervision is less miserable than being yelled at constantly but creates its own problems. There are all sorts of things that can delay the work. Tools break. We have to wait for someone else to use the forklift to get our materials up to the floor we're working on. Garbage is left where we're supposed to be working. The plans are wrong and we can't do things the easy way. All sorts of problems come up and we have to figure out how to get around them. The looser the supervision the more these are our problems. When the boss wants to know why something hasn't gotten done yet, we'll always bring up these technical problems—whether they're the real cause or not. This means that the boss who used to be a journeyman and went into business for himself is often the worst kind. He knows how long things should take and can tell what's a serious problem that should really cause a delay and when we're just using technical problems to cover up slacking off.

Another way for the company to keep us working hard is to pay piece wages. This is usually only done for jobs where it's easy to measure how much work is getting done. Drywallers will often have part of their wage tied to the number of sheets of drywall they put up. This gives them an incentive to work faster. Where some drywallers are

paid partially in piece rates and some on straight hourly wages, this creates a division between them. Some will try to go faster and others will try to go slower. The ones who want to go faster are often the more experienced workers and are often given some authority to supervise the other workers. Instead of being pushed directly, workers who get piece rates have an incentive to push themselves (and their coworkers) to go faster. The job is more stressful, since we have to worry about how fast we're working ourselves. It doesn't mean we're working for ourselves. It doesn't make the work less boring. It just changes the way that the pressure to work harder and faster is applied.

The fewer breaks we take, the faster we work, the more work we get done in a day, the more surplus value the company squeezes out of us. The faster we work, the more likely we are to have accidents or to get repetitive injuries. The harder we work, the more work is likely to eat up our free time. When we get home from work we'll be too tired to do anything but take a shower. The less time we spend talking to our coworkers, the more boring the work is. We push in the exact opposite direction as the company. We're constantly trying to slow down the pace of work as much as possible.

This requires a lot of coordination. We have to find ways to slow down even the workers who are friends with the boss or the new workers that we don't know and trust yet. If the foreman sees someone working slower than everyone else, they'll get yelled at and, if it keeps happening, fired. Since we often work in loosely supervised teams, the foreman doesn't know exactly who's working hard and who isn't. If one worker starts slacking off, the other workers he's working with will get mad at him because they're having to work harder to pick up his slack. No one likes a lazy individualist. A coordinated collective laziness is much better.

Often this happens without much thought going into it. A worker with more experience will find a lot of minor problems with the work of the new guy who's been downing energy drinks all day and working twice as hard as everyone else. This will slow him down to an acceptable rate. The culture on the job creates a standard for how much work we do and how much time we spend smoking, talking, hammering the wall pointlessly. A tone is set for all the workers on a job site, whether they've been explicitly told to "Slow the fuck down!" or not. Still, the stronger the work groups, the more ambitious we can be in slowing down the pace of work. On a job with lots of workers who trust each

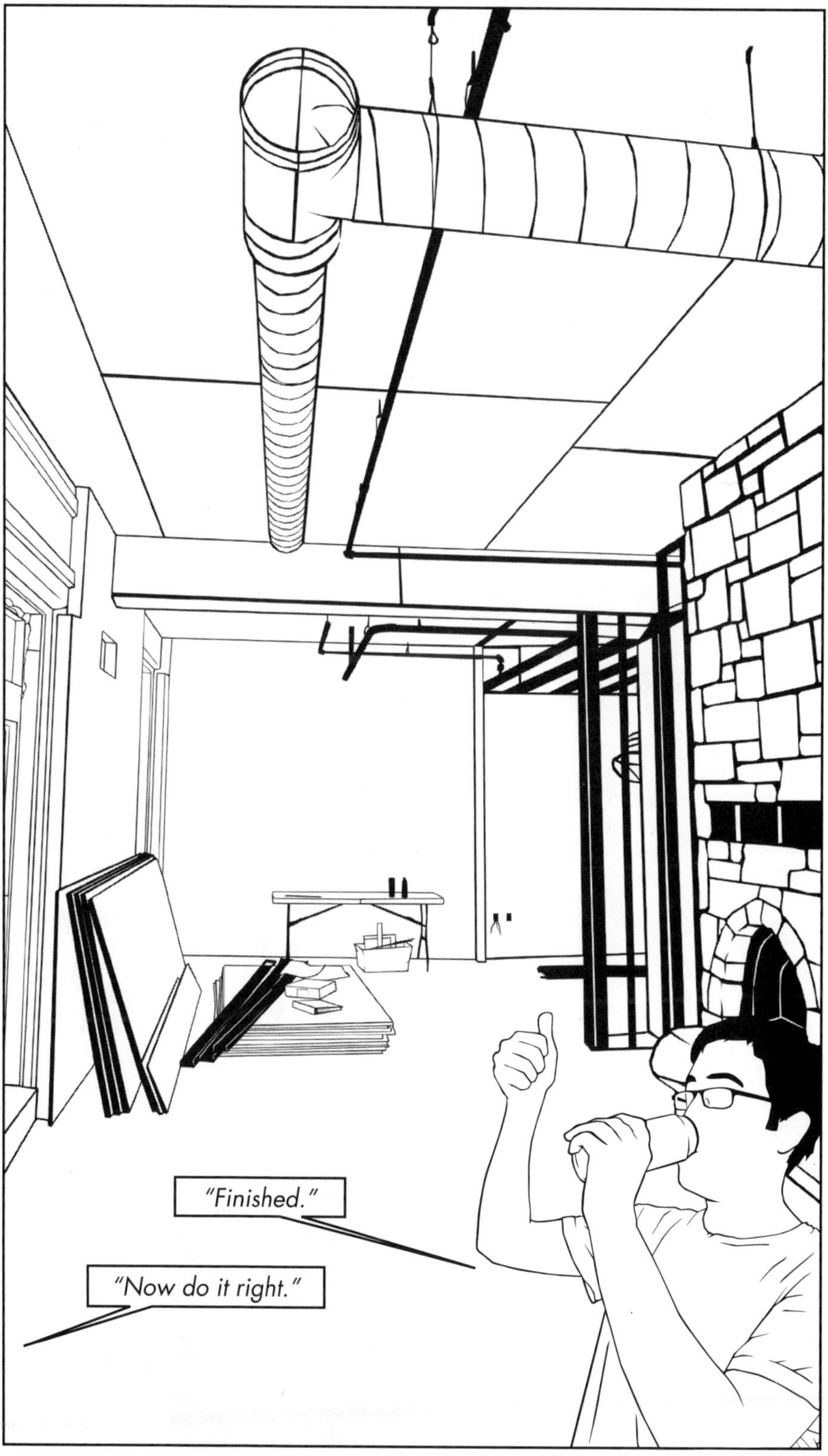
"Finished."
"Now do it right."

other and consciously plan together, we can slow the pace of work almost to a stop, and it's very hard for the boss to target any one worker as the lazy one or the troublemaker.

Depending on the balance of forces, the pace of work in a company at a specific construction site is somewhere between fast and intensely stressful and slow and exasperatingly boring.

No matter the pace of work, we're still at work. Sometimes, when we're completely unsupervised, we can cut out a couple hours early and say we worked a full day. Usually, though, we're stuck there, making shit for someone else to sell all day long. On a sunny day when there's no problems and we have some running jokes all day long, things fly by. We can be done before we know it. On a cold, rainy day when we have to work in the mud and keep running into problems and the foreman is yelling at us, it takes forever. Whichever it is, it's that part of our lives that we just want to be over. Slowing down the work doesn't necessarily make it go by faster. Sometimes the boss won't be there and we could sit around and do nothing, but instead we'll work just to make the time pass quicker. The boredom can really get to us. New construction workers quickly pick up the habit of talking to themselves. At first this is just to be able to think while people are driving dump trucks around or using nail guns right next to us. But it quickly becomes singing to ourselves, talking in strange voices, and doing imitations of the boss or various celebrities to create gaps in the boredom.

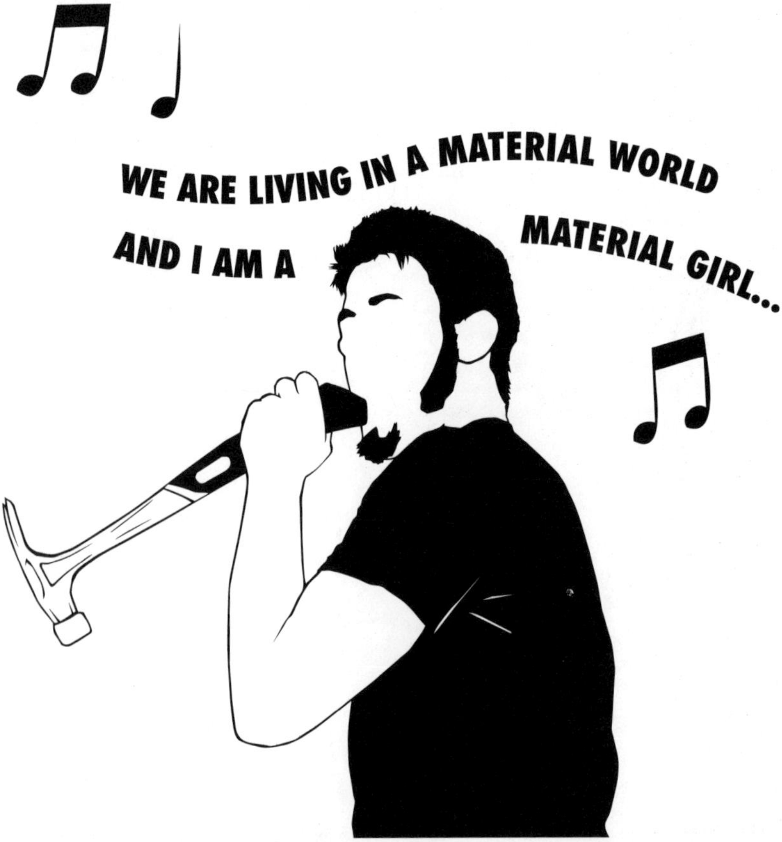
WE ARE LIVING IN A MATERIAL WORLD
AND I AM A
MATERIAL GIRL...

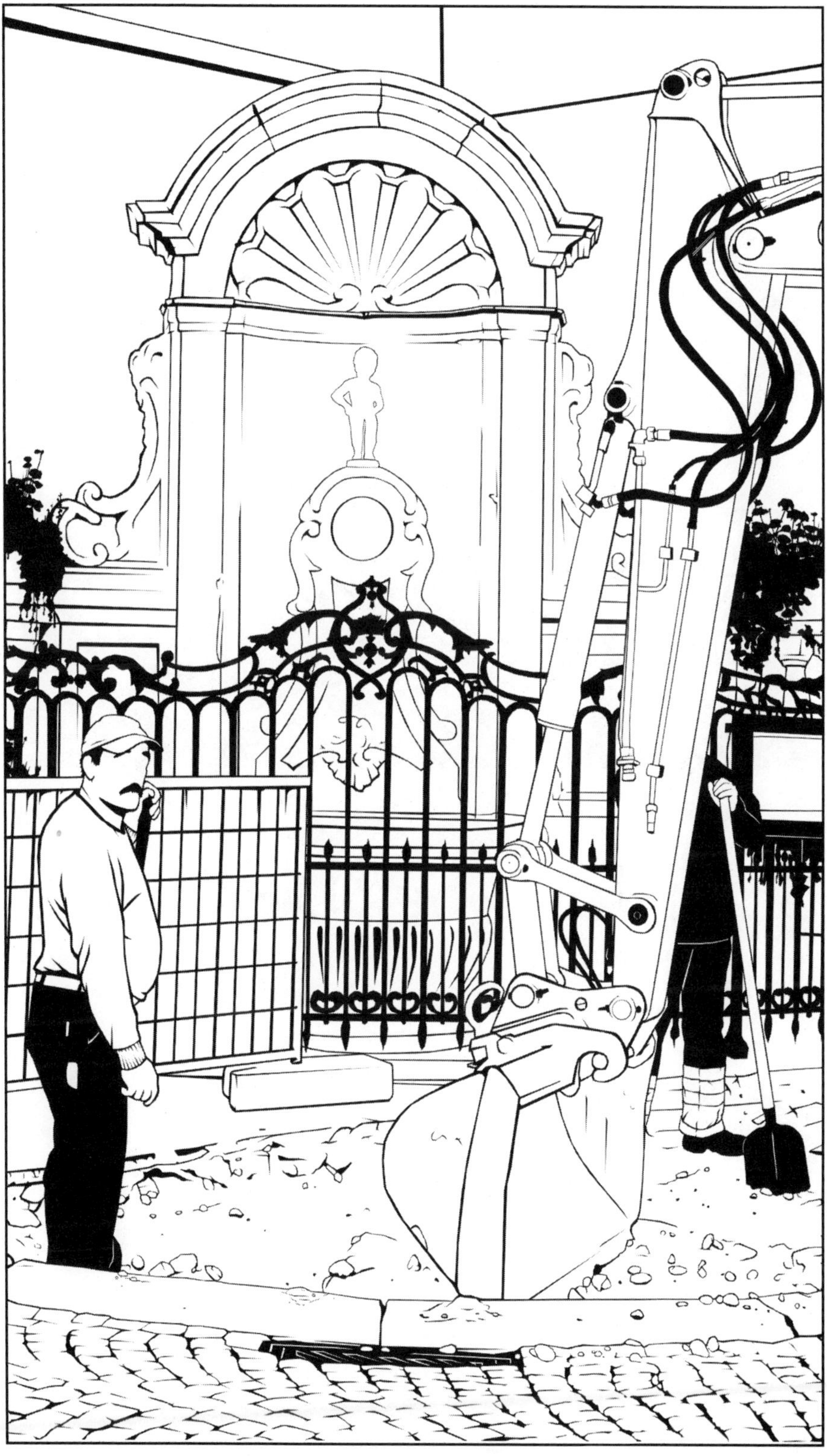

Safety and Self-Destruction

"I've never read Marx's Capital,
but I have the marks of capital all over me."

Bill Haywood

A construction site is a dangerous place. We're working on the edge of roofs, under heavy loads of material, next to gas pipes and live electrical lines, around heavy equipment and vehicles, with sharp power tools. Almost as many construction workers die or get injured on the job as miners, loggers, or prostitutes.

Safety costs money. Roofers have to be paid for the time they're setting up and putting on safety equipment, as well as the time they're actually putting up tar and shingles. Harnesses, carabiners, rope, hard hats, and goggles cost money. This means that there's always pressure on safety measures to be cut back in order to make more money for the company. This leads directly to accidents and deaths. Roofers fall and die because their boss was too cheap to buy safety harnesses. Parts of buildings collapse and kill the workers inside because the boss was cutting costs and using cheap materials.

Still, killing off your employees— especially hard-to-find, experienced employees—is not usually a viable business plan. For the good of the industry as a whole (and under pressure from the workers and consumer groups) the state imposes safety rules and regulations on construction companies. There

is a huge body of law that dictates exactly how and where different kinds of materials should be used to prevent fire, electrocution, and collapse. Government building inspectors have to repeatedly inspect and sign off on buildings at each stage of construction. The law also lays down rules about how work should be done, and which safety equipment is required for which tasks. Companies caught with serious safety violations can get huge fines or be shut down, which creates a counterweight to the incentive to skimp on safety to make more money. Sometimes general contractors will even have stricter safety policies than are required by law.

But the law is one thing, reality is another. Small contractors who work on individual homes rarely see safety inspectors and tend to have much lower standards of safety. Large contractors often have relationships with building inspectors,

and an inspector who knows a contractor will sometimes just sign off on a building without looking at it. He'd rather stand around and talk or go have a coffee than spend an hour carefully looking at everything. Safety laws are usually only closely enforced when the company has had accidents already. And the pressure to cut back on safety measures can't be legislated away.

A general contractor building a high-rise will require all the workers on the site to come to a safety meeting once a week. He'll lay down strict safety rules, give out (or sell) hard hats and safety goggles to anyone who needs them and tell everyone that they should report any safety violations they see. Then he'll call up the owner of the subcontracting company putting in the structural steel and tell him he needs to hurry up, or the building's skeleton won't be done on time. The boss comes down to the site the next day and tells the foreman he's not doing his job and he's got to push the guys harder. The foreman now tell the ironworkers to quit using harnesses when walking around on the beams because it takes too much

time and asks them to work overtime every day for a week. A bunch of sleep-deprived ironworkers are now walking around six stories up on thin steel beams without harnesses. If the general contractor has held safety meetings regularly and posted strict safety rules around the site, he's in a better position when he's sued by the family of the ironworker who falls to his death. Whatever the intentions of the individual capitalist with his money invested in house building, the need to cut costs and increase the pace of work itself undermines safety at a construction site.

But it's not just the boss who breaks safety rules. When the foreman is pushing us to get things done faster, it's often easier to cut back on safety procedures than to actually work harder. We'll reach dangerously out a window, rather than take all the time to put on a harness. A lot of safety regulations seem completely pointless. We know from experience better than the people who write the laws where and how to do the work safely. We usually see safety rules as more annoying than helpful, and resent

Construction is hard on the body. We breath in fumes from glues, paints, tar, as well as cement dust, wood chips, mold, and insulation. We get bruises, scrapes, cuts, burns, and splinters almost daily. The more repetitive the jobs the more likely we are to get repetitive strain injuries. If we've been working standing on a ladder all day, our feet will hurt. If we've been drilling all day or using power tools, we'll get shooting pains and numbness in our fingers. If we've been working low to the ground, our knees and back will be the source of the pain. At a construction site, bad backs are produced at almost the same rate as houses. The work of even the most skilled trades requires a lot of physical effort—and not the kind of physical effort that keeps you in shape. It's the kind that makes your body slowly disintegrate. Anyone can see how rough the work is by looking at the difference between a guy who's been a general contractor for decades and a guy who's been a laborer for the same amount of time.

The pain comes in on top of the boredom or the stress, and people have different ways of dealing. We take ibuprofen by the fistful and try to get our hands on stronger painkillers whenever possible. We quietly have a beer or two during breaks or subtly smoke pot out of a hollowed out hex screwdriver. This is officially frowned on for safety reasons. Workers caught drunk or high are kicked off the job and often fired. If we do have a serious accident and it's found that we were drunk or high, we can sometimes be denied workers' compensation.

Drugs are often unofficially tolerated, however. The general contractor pretends not to notice the flask in the forklift operator's coat pocket, because he knows that without it, his hands aren't steady. The boss takes aside one of his guys who's smoking weed and tells him "I don't care, but if you're caught

it when the general contractor yells at us for taking our hard hats off while smoking a cigarette next to the building.

Also, safety laws don't only target the boss. If a safety inspector sees an ironworker without a harness, the company will be fined, but also the ironworker will have to pay a fine (equal to a few days or maybe a week's wages). If he's caught with less immediately life-threatening safety violations, he might just be sent home for the day. This means that on most construction sites workers, foremen, and general contractors from different trades work together to get around safety rules. We'll warn each other if someone sees a safety inspector and temporarily follow all the rules until he's gone.

People die, fingers are chopped off, legs are crushed, eyes are cut up in spectacular accidents. Usually, though, the destruction of our bodies happens much slower. Safety is not usually our main concern.

you're on your own." Sometimes drugs even help get the job done quicker. A team of drywallers come in on the weekend, blast some dance music, take ecstasy, and do the whole job while rolling. When the ironworkers have to work overtime, the foreman gives them all a line or two of cocaine to keep them awake and motivated.

The addition of alcohol, marijuana, or other intoxicants to the already dangerous combination of power tools, heights and lack of sleep increases the danger of serious accidents at the same time it helps to alleviate the pain and boredom. The drugs help create a little distance from ourselves, as our bodies are steadily worn down.

This kind of self-destruction is not really thought out, but it does have a certain logic. The real horror of this logic can be seen when workers purposely injure themselves to get workers' compensation. Although this is very rare, the boss often suspects it. More common is that when we know, somewhere in a back corner of our mind, that if we get hurt, we'll get decent workers' compensation or disability pay, we take more risks at work. Our own activity at work is so miserable that self-destruction can seem like an alternative. More often, though, we just try to fake injuries or sickness, to get a few days off.

Injuries and accidents bring the class relation into sharp and infuriating contrast. When old, rusty scaffolding collapses and a worker dies, it's clear that the company's push to cut costs cost the worker his life. But it's no better if the company had the newest scaffolding and the best safety equipment. Management doesn't fall off roofs. We do. Even the good worker can't escape. He's worked hard, turned a screwdriver repetitively for thirty years, made a lot of money for the company and never had a major accident in his life. One morning he reaches for his coffee mug and his elbow just gives out—never to work right again.

Whether our bodies are used up slowly or quickly, whether our bosses are basically good guys who are trying to be safe or are greedy bastards who don't give a shit about their workers, the fact remains that we end up with injuries and health problems and they end up with profits.

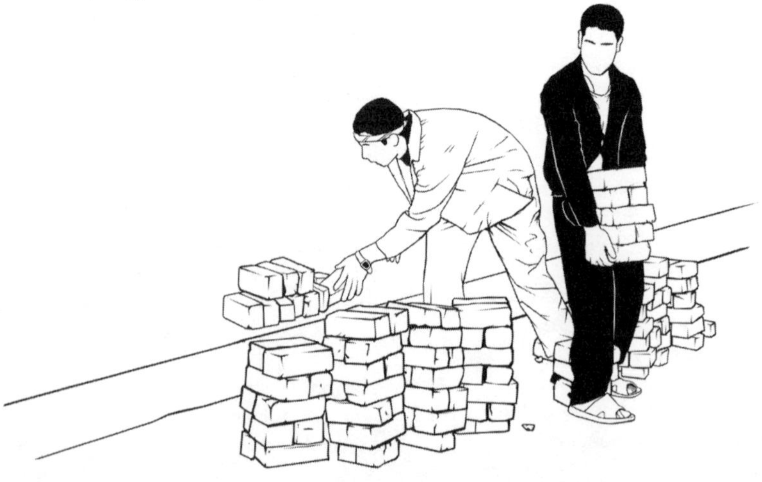

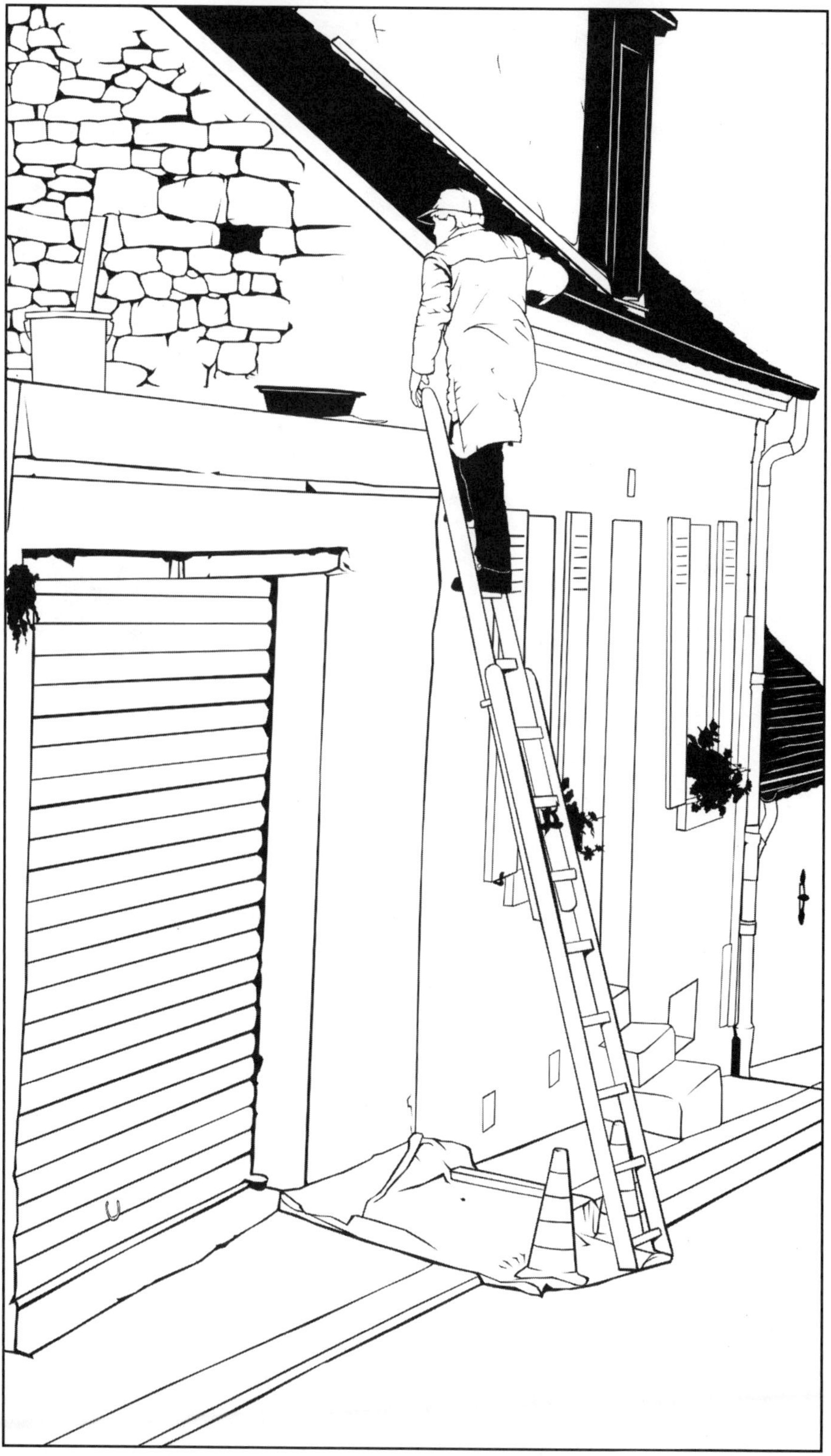

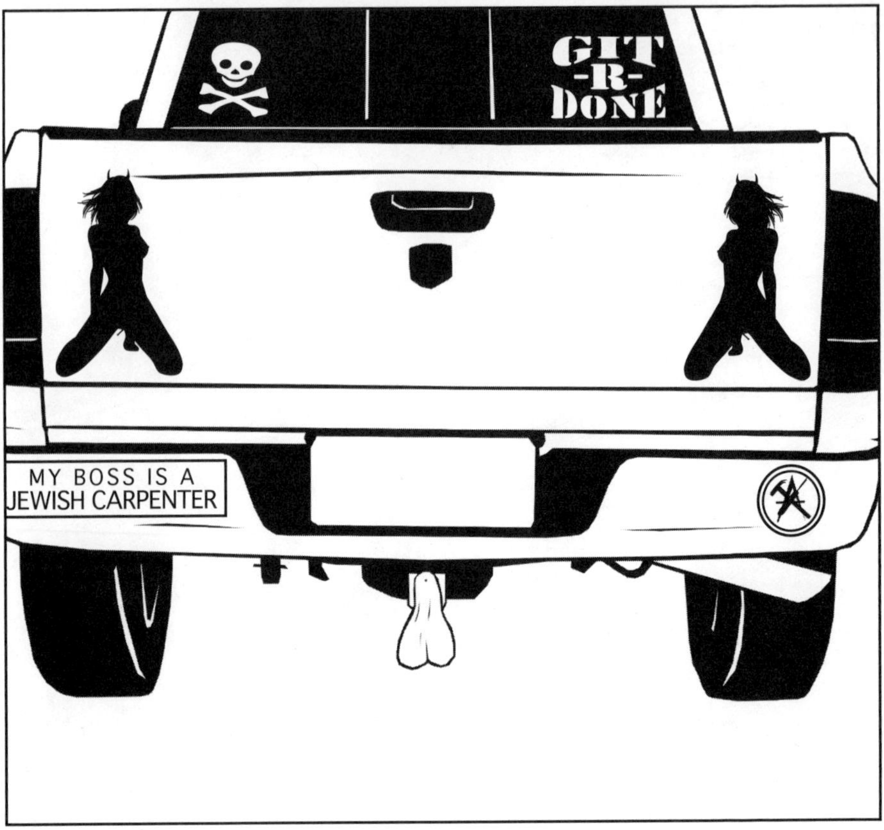
GIT
-R-
DONE
MY BOSS IS A
JEWISH CARPENTER

Macho Shit

"The assumption of one role after another,
provided he mimics stereotypes successfully,
is titillating to him. Thus the satisfaction derived from a well-played role
is in direct proportion to his distance from himself,
to his self-negation and self-sacrifice."

Raoul Vaneigem

high school boys' locker room. Things that would get you reprimanded in most workplaces (and lynched at a university) are common on a construction site.

Of course it's hard to be just one of the guys if you're a woman. Where the work culture is filled with macho shit it can make the lives of women workers absolutely miserable. Often the image of the sexist construction site is enough to keep women from even considering working in construction. The image reinforces the conditions it grows out of.

When a bunch of guys are together in the same place, often the first thing they talk about is women. Getting to know the new guy on the job often starts with asking about his woman. Everyone wants to see pictures of each other's wives and girlfriends—preferably naked ones. Talking about women is an easy way to socialize, because everyone's got something to say. (Openly gay construction workers are incredibly rare, but the old cliché that the most vocally homophobic guy on the site is a repressed homosexual is often obviously true.)

Just being one of the guys is a way to form some community, but it also shapes that community. The limited use of machines to replace tasks done by workers means that the work requires a lot of strength

T he macho construction worker is a widely recognized cliché. The construction site is often referred to (and denounced) as a model sexist workplace. Whether construction workers are more prejudiced than men working at hospitals, universities, or used car lots is an open question— a question that misses the point.

Construction work remains male. Although the number of women doing construction work has grown, women are still only a very small percentage of construction workers, and it's quite common for there to be no women at all on any given job. With no women around, construction sites can sometimes have the feel of a

Wanna see my caulk?

on the part of the worker. You have to be tough to do the work, and the fact that no one cares if you show up for work unshaven and with a black eye, adds to the image of toughness. Often an important part of getting the respect of the other workers is to prove that you're man enough to do the job. Being macho becomes part of the job—and being able to do the job makes you one of the guys. This happens more with the trades that are more dangerous and physical, like ironwork, but can happen in any construction job.

Being just one of the guys has its uses and appeal. Any time a moderately good-looking woman walks by the site it's time to take a break and check her out. Time spent talking about or checking out girls is time spent not working. Also, in addition to getting respect for skill and experience, we get respect for being hard. In this, only the electrician who broke his knee because he got his hand stuck on a feeder wire in the ceiling and had to kick out the ladder from under him is on the same level as the ironworkers.

Like racial or cultural communities, the identification based on playing the role of the macho construction worker creates a community that includes the workers and the boss. Unlike racial or cultural communities, it doesn't function on a construction site to divide the workers against each other, for the simple reason that there are very few women construction workers. It works, but not by playing men and women workers against each other.

Being a tough guy is not mainly about admiring the developer's assistants' tits or talking about which of the girls who work at the bar down the road you'd like to fuck. Being a tough guy means working on live electrical wires (rather than stopping work to go down to the electrical room and turn them off). It's not bothering with safety equipment. It's working overtime any time the boss needs you. It's continuing to work when you're injured and not complaining about it. It's lifting heavy materials yourself rather than getting someone else to help with them. Macho shit is profitable. We do things that make the boss more money and are directly against our own interests. All we get in return is the respect of being "one tough motherfucker."

Imaginary respect compensates for real lack of respect and machismo becomes an ideology.

Although it can be very useful for the boss, a macho atmosphere doesn't exist on every construction site. In order to keep up the atmosphere and to be just one of the guys, the boss and the foreman have to play along. This means lifting heavy shit and doing dangerous jobs themselves, rather than always getting us to do them—obviously an unattractive prospect.

Also, in companies where men and women work together and do the same jobs, this kind of machismo loses its coherence. The ability to do the job stops being a sign of being a real man, and the social side of a bunch of guys standing around talking about girls loses its connection to working hard and being tough—it stops being profitable. A machismo that includes women is not impossible, but a far weaker ideology.

Still, construction companies that employ lots of women are rare, and being a construction worker continues to mean being one of the guys. In this atmosphere, the women who do work for any length of time in construction tend to be tough, competent, and to have a lot of balls.

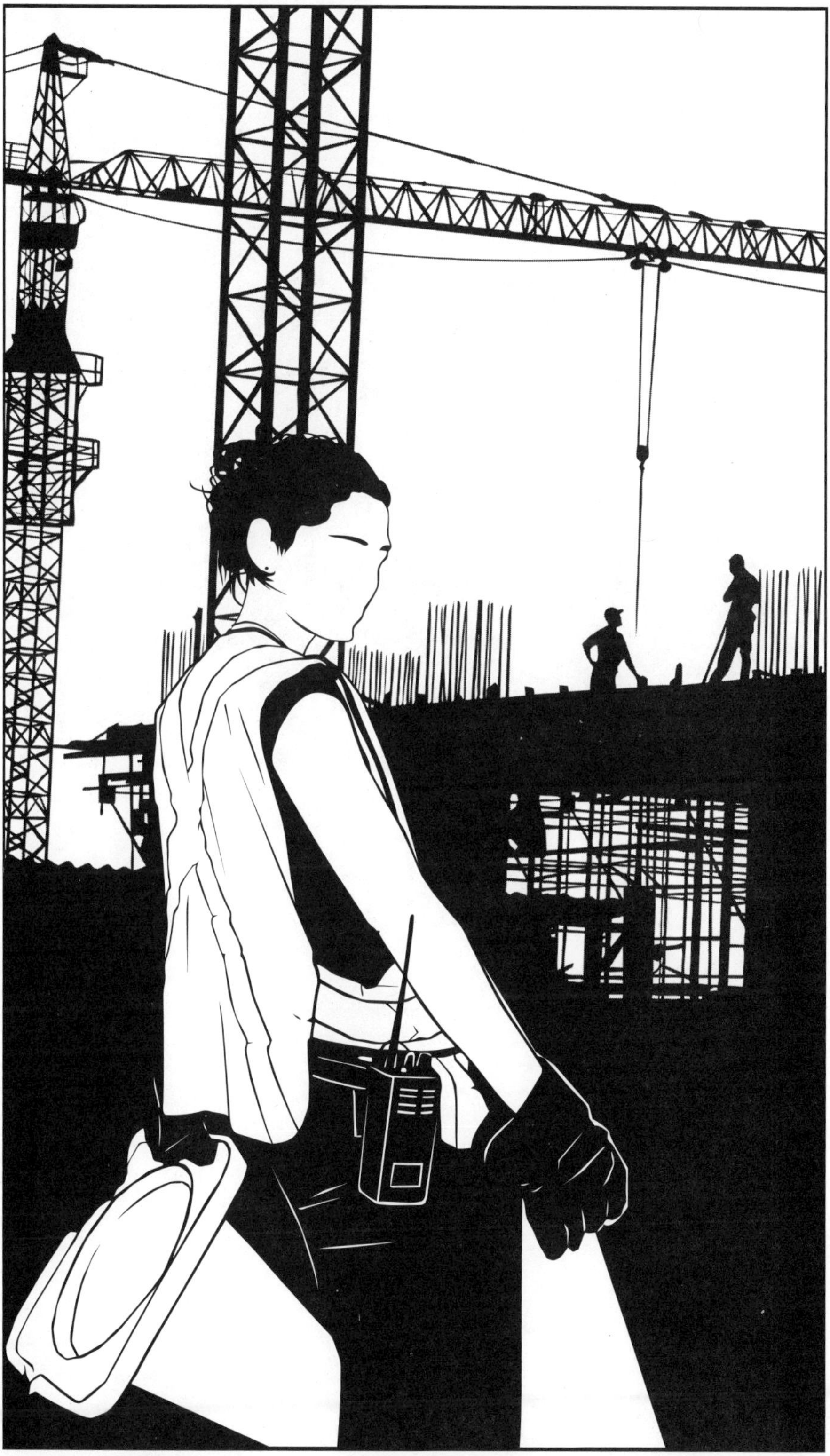

Blue-Collar Blues

*"It's a big job just gettin' by with nine kids and a wife
but I've been a workin' man dang near all my life,
and I'll keep on workin', long as my two hands are fit to use.
I'll drink my beer in a tavern, sing a little bit of these workin' man blues."*

Merle Haggard (from "Workin' Man Blues")

With nothing to sell but our ability to work, we are dependent on finding a buyer. But we can't separate our ability to work from ourselves when we sell it. We, unfortunately, have to be there, although the time in contrast. When we're unemployed this need to spend our free time fades away, and we tend to become lethargic—partially because we have no money to go out, but also because the contrast doesn't exist anymore.

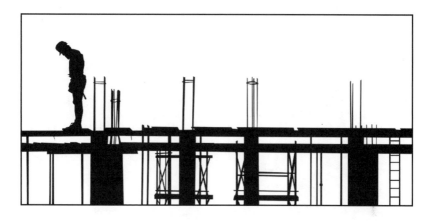

is no longer our own. Our activity at work is not an expression of our lives but something separate from them. We have to spend our time working for someone else to be able to exist on our own time. We both need and hate the work.

We find all sorts of ways of dealing with this contradiction.

With work eating up most of our time, we try to cram as much into our free time as possible. We'll get completely wasted on Friday after work, go to the movies, go out to eat, go to the game, try to get ourselves as worn out as possible. Although work is separated from the rest of our lives, the need to make sure that work time is a filled with as much work as possible creates, on the other side, a need to make sure that leisure time is filled with as much leisure as possible. And of course the more expensive things we do in our free time, the more we'll have to work to afford them. We feel cheated if we just rest up on the weekend. Even when we're not specifically commuting to work or washing our work clothes, work time shapes free time, although the two can only exist

Another way to cope is try to convince ourselves that we don't mind the job. On a nice summer day when we're covered in mud and insulation we'll tell ourselves, "at least I'm not stuck in an office."

redneck girl

work hard
play hard

When the foreman's yelling at us we'll say, "at least I don't have to deal with customers."

Sometimes this even works. Anyone who does the same job for a long time has to take some interest in it or go insane. We are proud of our abilities even if they get used up in pointless ways.

This pride or attachment to our work can be the basis for a positive, almost respectable identity. Although officially anyone can become a rock star or a politician, unofficially everyone knows this isn't true. That vast majority of us will spend most of our lives trading our lives for a wage. Our only asset is our ability to work, and we develop a view of ourselves based on that. During an election, there is a certain appeal when politicians talk about how the average Joe works hard and still gets no respect and can barely make ends meet.

As being working-class becomes an officially recognized identity it becomes a stereotype of itself. The workin' man does manual labor, likes his religion, his porn, his sports, his shitty beer, and his unhealthy food. The workin' woman is the same but is a stay-at-home mom, or works as a waitress, a hairdresser, or a secretary and likes women's magazines and rom-coms instead of porn and sports. These images grow out of reality but also impose themselves back on that reality. The working class becomes a sociological category (or several) defined by income and lifestyle choices, which can then be marketed to by businesses and pandered to by politicians.

It's not that a broader, more inclusive image of what it means to be working-class would be less exploitative—a female (or a transgendered) construction worker who eats organic, vegetarian food can be put to work and have surplus value sucked out of her, just like a male construction worker who eats

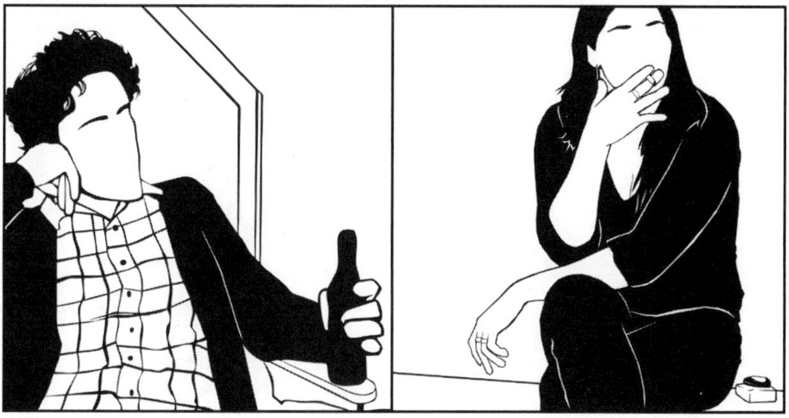

hamburgers. Capital can tolerate any number of identities and lifestyles and make money off them. It's not representations themselves that are the problem. Everyone develops some kind of images of their lives and their work. Without some images and representations of what it is to be working-class, we would all feel like failures and hate ourselves for not being movie stars, professional athletes, supermodels, and CEOs.

Blue-collar identity institutionalizes a certain resentment of the rich. The poor worker does all the work, while the rich make obscene profits. Our daily struggle to survive is glorified. It is a positive identity based on the very thing that we hate: the fact that we're forced into wage labor. Politics built on this identity (like all identity politics) are inherently conservative. A pathetic moral superiority and resentment take the place of an ability to change our situation. It is the ideology of the wage laborer who can't imagine any way out of wage labor.

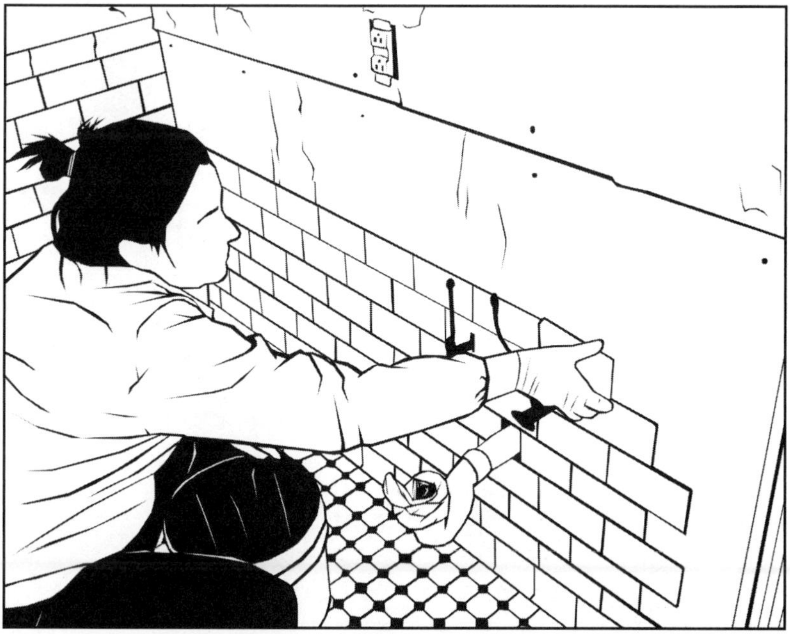

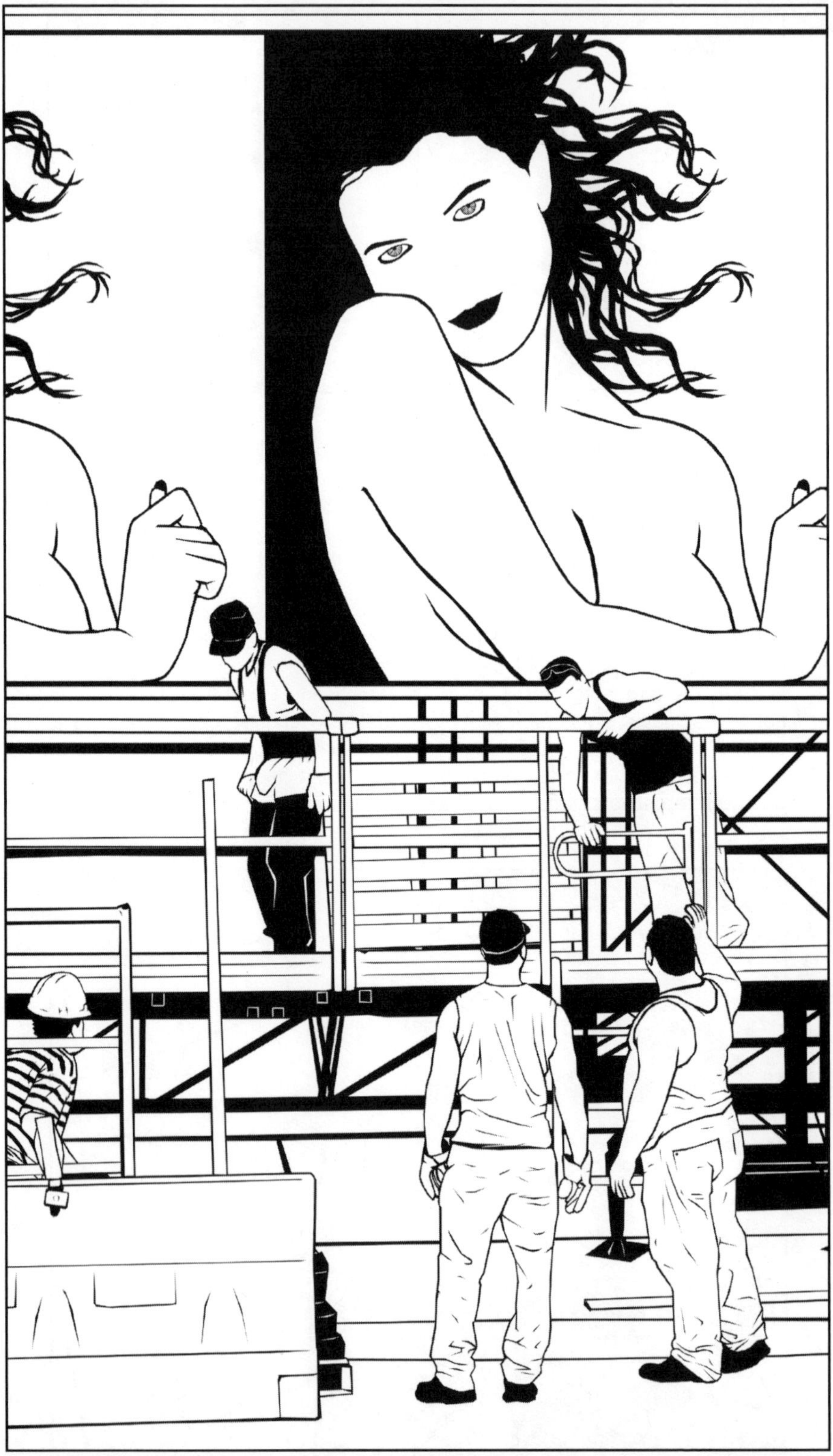

But ideology and action are not the same thing. No matter how fatalistic or unimaginative we get, the hatred of work and the desire to escape from it come out. An older worker takes a certain pride in explaining something to a new apprentice. At the same time, he tells him to go look for a different, better job.

We often have to lie, bargain and negotiate with ourselves to get out of bed every morning. The guy who's been complaining about how he needs to make some more money finally gets some overtime and works all weekend. Then he spontaneously calls in sick Monday and Tuesday, almost canceling out the overtime.

It's not blue-collar pride that keeps us going to work every day. Class is a social relationship, not an identity. Every day we work, we make houses, but we also reproduce that relationship. The company makes a profit and once again the boss needs to hire us to keep his capital in motion. We end up with a wage and, once again, no way to make money but to sell our ability to work to someone else. We are recreated as workers. This class relationship is the starting and ending point of capitalist production. Different images are associated with different kinds of wage labor. We want to stop being working-class.

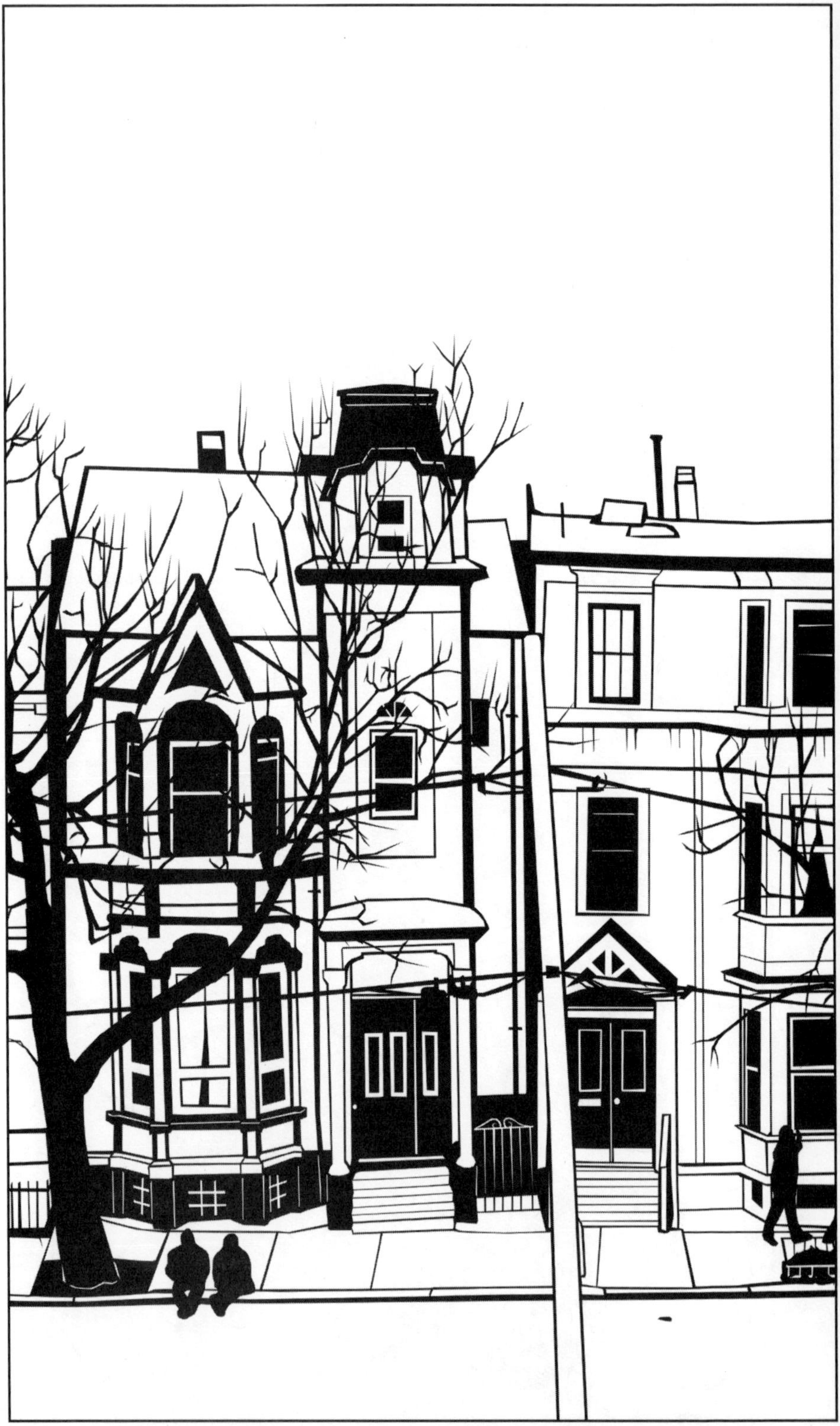

THE NEIGHBORHOOD

"Hunger is hunger, but the hunger gratified by cooked meat eaten with a knife and fork is a different hunger from that which bolts down raw meat with the aid of hand, nail and tooth. Production thus produces not only the object but also the manner of consumption..."

Karl Marx

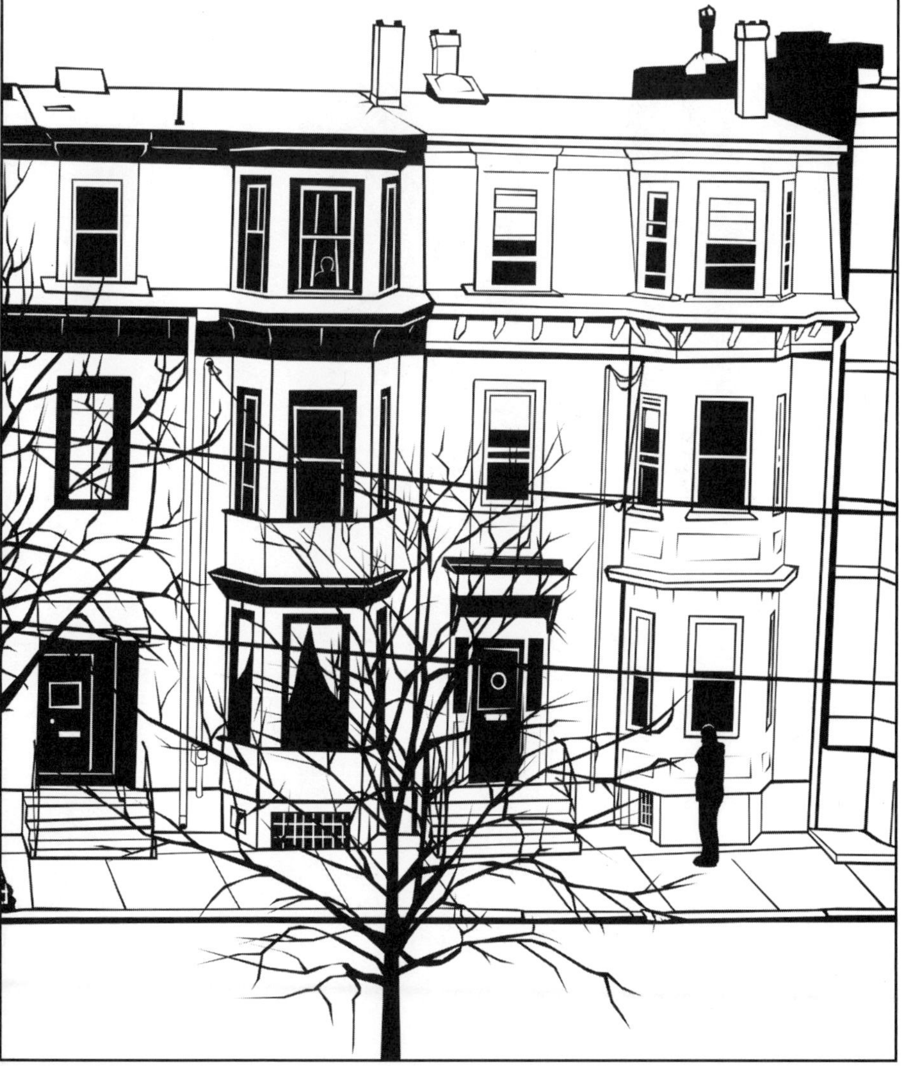

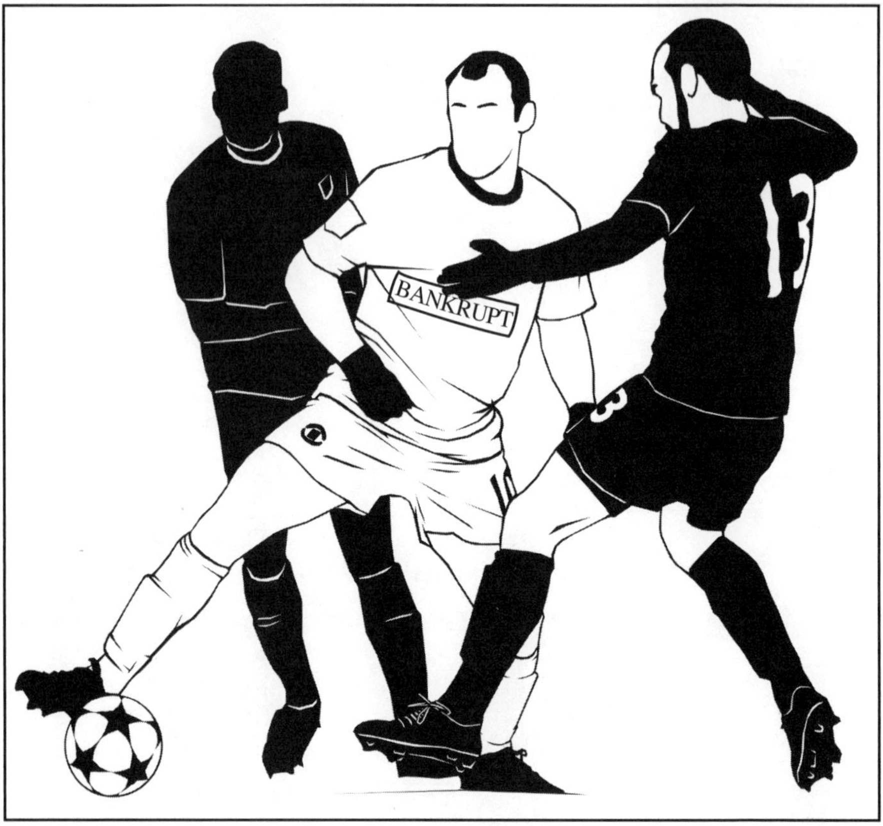
BANKRUPT

Loans

"When the biggest, richest, glassiest buildings in town are the banks, you know that town's in trouble."

Edward Abbey

Houses are produced for a profit by building contractors at a construction site. But the contractors are not the only, or the most influential, businessmen involved in house construction. More often than not, a contractor borrows money to cover his expenses and a capitalist in the business of giving out loans gets involved.

The construction contractor borrows money—from a bank for example. He uses this to buy materials, machines and to hire workers. The machines and materials are used up (slowly or quickly transferring their value to the house) and our work adds more value to the house than we are paid in wages. The contractor sells this for more than his investment and makes a profit. The profit then has to be divided into two parts. Part of it he keeps, and part of it he has to hand over to the bank in the form of interest.

The division of the profits between the profit a capitalist gets from actually running the business, and interest on loans happens according to a general interest rate for similar loans in the market. The riskier the loan looks, the higher the interest rate, the more of the profit the lender takes. The interest rate moves up and down in response to conditions in the larger economy and the balance of supply of and demand for loan money.

The business of loaning does not create value but is useful for the businesses who do. Credit allows the separation of buying and selling in time. A contractor can buy raw materials on credit and pay for them later when he's used them to make a profit. This means a contractor doesn't have to wait until he has been paid for his last job to start a new job. His capital can be kept constantly in motion, and the time his machinery is sitting around rusting is kept to a minimum. The circuit of capital can be sped up.

financial capitalist
loan money
industrial capitalist
commodities
production
commodities worth more
more money
profit
profit of enterprise
repaid loan money
interest

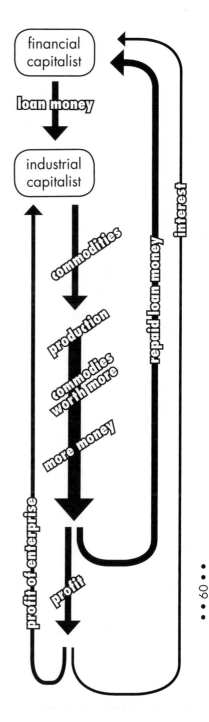

Money

more Money

Having specialized loan capitalists also means that people with good ideas about how to squeeze surplus value out of us, but not a lot of startup capital, can try their ideas out. Banks don't just give out loans, they also borrow. They borrow money from each other, and every time anyone deposits money in the bank, they are lending money to the bank. Banks make money by paying less in interest than they charge. At the same time, they channel money from deposits into loans to businesses— they turn savings into capital.

When a bank loans out money to a general contractor, it can be used by him as real capital, to buy building materials, hire workers, and produce houses for sale. What the bank gets in return is the right to have the contractor pay back the loan with interest. This is a file on a computer somewhere (probably with a paper backup). It goes nowhere near a construction site. The bank can't hire a bunch of workers to create more rights to collect interest. Its value can't be based on the amount of work time necessary to create it. Other ways of pricing it have to be found if it is going to be treated as capital and sold. This is done by dividing interest payments by the interest rate. If a bank is getting $50,000 a year in interest payments on a bundle of

loans, and the annual rate of interest is 5%, the bank's accountants will treat this flow of money as the interest on a capital worth $1 million. (With the same payments, but an interest rate of 10%, the loans would be priced at $500,000). The capitalized loans can then be sold and traded on the market. They have a price, but their value is imaginary. They are not real commodities being produced, only a claim to a cut of the future profits of the business that originally took out the loan. The movements of stock markets we hear about every day on the radio or see ticking across the bottom of the TV news are movements of this imaginary capital.

For the capitalist who runs a construction business, increasing his capital means building houses. From the point of view of the loan capitalist, any business is as good as the next. He loans out money and gets back more money. All he cares about is the rate of interest. Although his profit is ultimately based in the production of value, it has lost its connection to real things being produced and sold. Capital seems like money that expands all by itself, and any stream of money is treated as the interest on some amount of capital. So long as he's confident he will get his money back with interest, the banker doesn't care if the money he lends out is used

$$\frac{\text{interest payments}}{\text{interest rate}} = \text{price of loan}$$

to invest in a business that makes real commodities, or is used to buy a house, a yacht, to put on a fireworks show, or to pay off earlier loans.

Since shares, like capitalized loans, are claims on future value (and have no value in themselves), anyone buying them has to anticipate, guess, bet, speculate about the future profitability of the firms they

transactions, and security guards to stand around bored. They are a monument to how financially sound the bank itself is.

So long as businesses keep growing steadily, they can pay off their loans. Imaginary capital accumulates and helps real capital to accumulate. Banks are willing to loan money and interest rates don't get out

represent. What an individual, a bank, or a corporation is worth becomes a question of opinion. The price of a stock begins to include all sorts of assumptions about what the future of the company (and the world it does business in) will be like. This kind of speculation helps move capital quickly from companies whose business plans looks weak to different more profitable-looking companies, or to completely different industries. It becomes very important for large corporations to appear to be as solid as possible. The headquarters of a large bank are not just a place for tellers to process

of control. Speculators bid up share prices, betting the economy will keep growing (often using borrowed money to do this). The prices of commodities being speculated on seem to lose any connection to how much work time it takes to make them. Money multiplies and profits seem to come out of thin air. The market seems miraculous.

But miracles don't exist. When the crash inevitably comes, last year's (or last week's) confidence looks like stupidity. Prices that had built-in assumptions of a profitable future pop or deflate like balloons. A small loss to a company that was speculating using borrowed money can easily mean bankruptcy. Debt defaults cascade through the system. Investors look for the safest investments. Nobody wants to loan out money except at very high interest rates. Nobody wants to buy claims on the future value produced by businesses currently in trouble, which drives their shares can only be sold by dropping their prices. The connections linking the various steps that capital has to move through to accumulate snap.

During a crisis the capitalists remember that value is something more than just the point where the supply and demand curves meet— that it depends on putting real people to work. An economic crisis is a crisis

down further and puts them in worse trouble. And the rising interest rate itself drops the prices of capitalized loans. Large amounts of imaginary capital simply disappear. In the real economy, capital finds it harder to go through its regular circuits. Businesses find that they can't sell their commodities and therefore can't pay back their loans. Businesses who regularly need loans and credit can't get them except at unprofitable interest rates, and they are forced to slow down their production and lay off workers or hack away at wages. This drop in demand hurts the businesses who usually sell them their raw materials, tools, and machines. These businesses then find they have produced too many commodities for the market. Part of their capital gets tied up in unsold commodities, which

of value production. It's not that real people don't need real houses. There is homelessness and people living in overcrowded houses. It's not that there aren't enough people around with the skills to build houses, or that there aren't enough raw materials or machines to build houses. Construction workers are out of work, machines are rusting, nails and two-by-fours are sitting in warehouses. They are not brought together because they can't be brought together profitably—just as they would be brought together to build things that have no relation to real need (like advertising billboards) if it could be done profitably. The economy recognizes only effective demand—needs backed up by money.

With weaker companies going out of business, there is more room in the market for the stronger ones. Wage cuts lower the price of our ability to work, and unemployment increases the labor supply and makes us willing to take jobs for less pay. Overstocked commodities get sold off cheaply. The businesses that survived the storm are now in a position to take advantage of these opportunities to produce

to him that he does all the hard work (of exploiting the workers), while the banker and the investor just sit back and slurp off money. Occasionally businessmen will even promote the (already widespread) hatred of bankers and stock market traders, and try to mobilize public support for regulations to cut down on speculation.

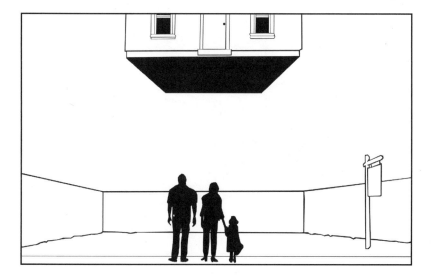

profitably again. Their capital begins to regain some of the value it had lost. Eventually confidence starts to recover, investments and loans begin to come back, the interest rate begins to drop, and a recovery can begin. The cycle is set to start all over again.

Credit, loans, imaginary capital and speculation grow out of the needs of businesses producing and selling real commodities, but react back on those businesses and cause them problems, especially during an economic crisis. From the point of view of a businessman who has loans to pay off, the banker can seem like a kind of parasite. The division of profits between interest and the profits from running an enterprise makes the capitalist running a business feel like a worker, compared to the investors and bankers. It seems

The building industry is extremely sensitive to the cycles of boom and bust in the economy. Movements of interest rates affect house prices doubly. Not only do builders take out loans when producing houses, but everyone except the super-rich takes out a loan when they buy a house. This makes the construction industry especially unstable—producing very quickly during an upswing and stopping completely during a downturn. During the height of a boom, construction workers might be working seven twelves. After a crash we may be out of work for months at a time. Also, since housing loans are so widespread, the simple home mortgage loan is an important part of the foundation on which the whole international financial system is built.

Land

"Buy land. They're not making it anymore."

Mark Twain

In order to run any business, it has to be run somewhere, on some piece of land. This means that a capitalist in the business of buying, selling, or leasing land gets involved. Since construction takes place only once on each spot and then has to move to a new location, the price of the land the house is built on is very important, and the landowner is extremely influential on when, where, and how houses are built.

But landowners deal with all sorts of businessmen, not just those running construction companies. Compare two small commercial capitalists—corner stores owners. They start with money (or a loan), buy potato chips, chewing gum, halal sodas, beer, cigarettes, and lottery tickets to stock their store, and hire a couple workers to run the cash register. They then resell these things

transferring the titles of ownership (of the various commodities in the store). The corner store owners buy cheaper than market price and take some of the surplus value produced when soda is produced, which they get as profit when they resell it. By acting as middlemen and buying the soda from the soda factory, the owner of the soda factory doesn't have to wait around until all the soda reaches its end users, before he reinvests that money in production. The corner stores help speed up the movement of capital invested in soda production (and beer production and potato chip production etc.) and keep them each from having to run their own stores. The cashiers in the corner store have the same relationship to their boss that a productive worker would—the harder he can get them to work, and the less money he pays

for more money. The cashiers may do the odd productive task, such as maintenance, and moving products around, but for the most part they are unproductive. They don't produce or transform commodities and add value to them; they just work

them, the more money he makes. So far, the two corner stores are exactly the same.

For both corner stores, an important business expense is renting the storefront. The landlord loans the store owner a piece of land with a

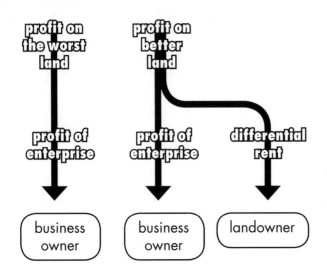

```
profit on          profit on
the worst          better
land               land

profit of          profit of          differential
enterprise         enterprise         rent

business           business           landowner
owner              owner
```

building on it and expects money in return. The building itself has a value based on how much time it takes to make it. The landlord will expect a regular payment for the loss of value to the building caused by wear and tear from regular use, as well as a regular rate of profit on his investment in the building. But there is also the price of the land itself. Except in extremely odd cases, land is not built, and therefore land prices cannot be based on the amount of work time necessary to make a piece of land. Still, the price of the land itself is usually far more important in determining the cost of renting a storefront than the price of buildings (although in practice they are both part of the regular rent payments and can't be separated).

Say one corner store is located in the worst possible place where someone can run a corner store and still make a profit, and the other corner store is located on a busy street in a major city. The city has universities, museums, sports stadiums, hospitals, jobs, a transportation system, tourist attractions. All these mean that there will be a lot more people walking by the big-city corner store than the worst-located corner store. The big-city corner store owner is going to be able to sell things faster and therefore have a higher rate of profit. Just the fact that he is doing business in a different (and better) place means he makes extra profits. The landlord can then take these extra profits in the form of rent.

To the extent that the landlord takes these extra profits and no more, having a separate group of capitalists in the land business is useful to business as a whole. If there was no rent taking away the extra profits from different locations, no one would bother to invest in businesses that weren't in the best locations, and businesses with the best locations would be under no competitive pressure and could make a profit very easily. By taking away the extra profits as rent, the landowning capitalists force the capitalists actually running businesses to compete with each other. A new machine or way of organizing the work that speeds up buying and selling at the worst corner store will make it more profitable than a big-city one, and all corner stores will have to start using the innovation.

But there's no guarantee that the landlord will just take these extra profits (created by the difference between the land he's renting out and the worst land). Even the landlord who owns the worst location for a corner store, will demand some rent. The land business is a business, not a charity. The land business is also different from other businesses. If there is a high demand for stripey scarves, and only a few stripey scarf factories, the price of stripey scarves will rise. The existing stripey scarf factories will see their rate of profit rise. Capital will be taken out of industries with a low rate of profit (starting with plain-colored scarf factories) and invested in stripey scarf production. As more capital moves into the stripey scarf business, the supply will rise and the price will fall and the rate of profit will fall toward the average. But land can't be produced like stripey scarves. A businessman who wants to become a landlord can't simply build new land and rent it out. There is only so much land and it already has owners. Private property in land is a monopoly. It is a barrier to investment, to the free flow of capital. This means that even owners of the worst land in use will get rent payments, and a part of any rent has nothing to do with the advantages that the land brings. The extra value taken in rent in this way might be produced by the business using the land (if the business invests more money in living labor than dead labor compared to the average) or it might come from value produced elsewhere in society (if the product created on the land is sold at a high monopoly price). This means that the interests of the landowner and the interests of the capitalists producing and selling commodities, can come into conflict with each other.

Ownership of the land is ownership of the right to collect rent payments from the land. When a landlord loans his land out to a corner store owner, he is expecting a cut of the corner store owner's future profits. If a new subway line is built with a stop near the corner store, this will bring more people by the corner store, and the landlord will raise the rent. If a new book about the city gets internationally popular and people come from all over the world to visit the city (and therefore pass by the corner store), the landlord will raise the rent. Private property in land is a social relationship between the landowner and other capitalists—the landowner profits off development and progress in society without having to do anything to contribute to it.

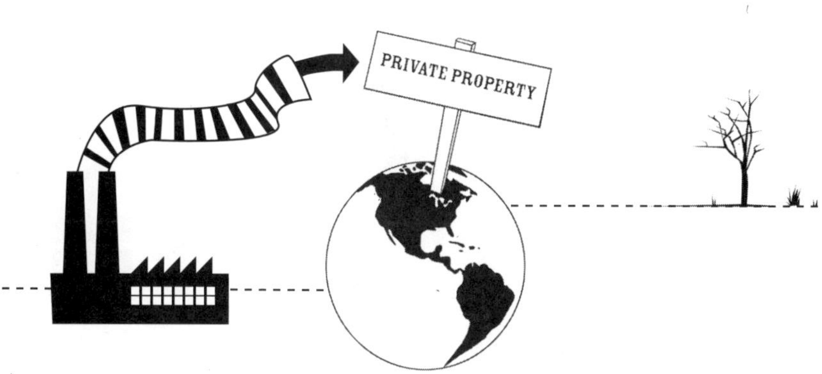
PRIVATE PROPERTY

Like all good loan capitalists, the landlord doesn't care what the capital is used for. So long as he is confident that he'll get regular rent payments, he doesn't care if the tenant is a business producing and selling real commodities, a political party that needs a storefront headquarters, a union that needs a meeting room, a band that needs a practice space, or a family that needs a place to live. Whether or not the land is used to produce value, the landowner treats the rent as his profit. In order to have some shelter, we have to buy it from a landed capitalist. In this case the same economic arrangement—paying rent—hides a different social relationship. Private property in land means that landowners get to charge us a fee for the right to live on earth.

barriers to development
barriers to development
barriers to development

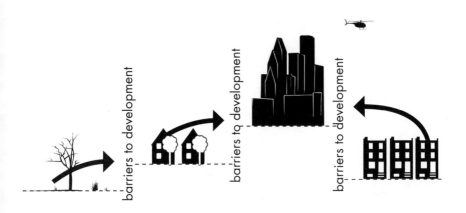

The right to collect rent payments can be capitalized and sold like a loan. If a piece of land at an intersection in a city can be expected to be rented out for $10,000 a year, and the annual rate of interest is 10%, the landlord would treat this rent as the interest payment on a capital of $100,000. Rising rents lead to rising land prices. Falling interest rates lead to rising land prices. But the right to collect rent does not have value in itself. If it is bought and sold, it is imaginary capital. It is the right to a cut of the future profit produced on that land. This means that land prices usually have built-in assumptions about the uses the land will be put to and the future of the neighborhood, the city, and the world the land is located in. Land markets are filled with speculation.

Land rents (and therefore land prices) are very different depending on what the land is used for. Agricultural land is cheaper than land used to build brick row houses to rent to the urban poor. Land used to build luxury condominiums is more expensive than either but cheaper than the land on which a skyscraper is going to be built as offices for banks, law firms, or insurance companies. There may be zoning laws that regulate which land can be used for stores, factories, houses, parks, and agriculture. The stronger these laws, the more separate the different land markets, but the bigger the difference between the rates of rent possible from different land uses, the more pressure will be put on the laws to change.

It's in the landowner's interest to use their land in the most profitable way, but if the land is owned by the business operating on it, they are not usually quick to respond to new potential uses. The businessman who owns a corner store and the

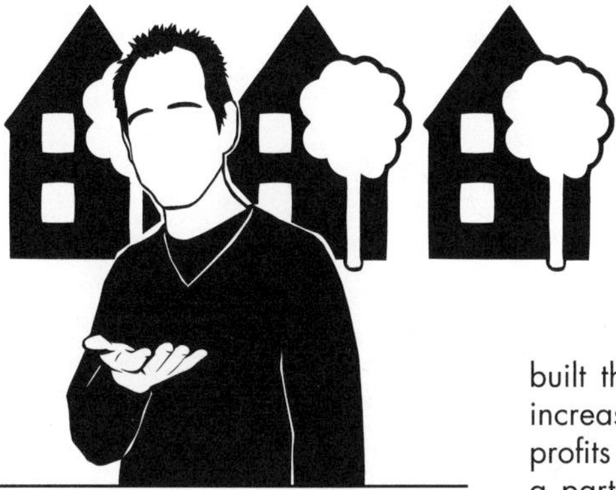

lot the corner store is located on might notice that the neighborhood is growing and people with more money to spend are moving in. He might stock some new, more expensive items. He's not going to be quick to go lobby the city council to rezone his lot so he can build luxury condominiums.

A separate group of land speculators are useful here, because they promote the most profitable use of the land. They bid up the price of the land, anticipating its future use. Cornfields at the edge of a growing city start to be more expensive because it is thought that a suburban neighborhood could be built there. A parking lot in downtown sells for a killing because an office tower could be built there. To the extent that these increased prices take away extra profits caused by the advantages of a particular location, they increase competition and can be good for business in general. To the extent that they create monopoly prices, landed capital becomes a drain on commercial and industrial capital.

If oil traders rarely fund the bombing of oil refineries to create political instability and increase the anticipated future price of oil, if gold speculators only try to bomb Fort Knox in the movies, land speculators are rarely content to sit back and passively hope that rent on the land they own will rise. They take an active role in development.

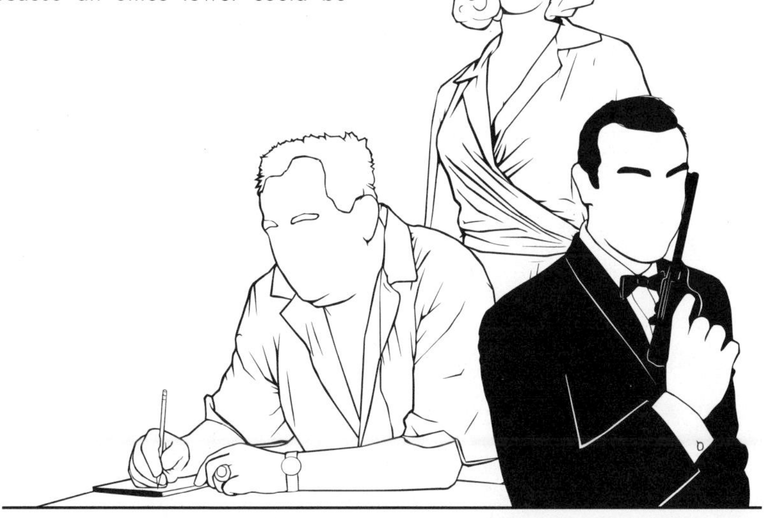

Development and Decay

"He does not care who lives in the room at the top provided he owns the building..."

Christopher Logue

The construction industry is closely tied to growth in the larger economy. For houses to be produced and sold, interest rates on mortgages and loans to contractors have to be kept under control. Also, since it takes a long time for houses to wear out, a lot of the demand has to come from an expanding market—not from replacing old houses. But the building industry's expansion and contraction does not just mean that commodities get sold or pile up in warehouses somewhere. The growth or stagnation of the building industry is visible in the development and decay of the neighborhoods we live in.

This reshaping of a neighborhood is pushed forward (and often completely dominated) by developers, not the construction contractors and subcontractors. Developers buy plots of land to build on, borrow money to finance building, get the building permits and zoning changes from the city, and organize the sale of the houses later for more money. The various ways that development companies are organized lead to different kinds of building practices and different kinds of neighborhoods.

The economic boom in the United States after the Second World War created sustained demand for housing and allowed for the creation of huge development firms. One of the largest was run by William Levitt. It was both a development firm and a construction company, and it also had its own concrete factories, nail factories, and lumber yards. Levitt built on a large scale, developing whole neighborhoods at once. This allowed for standardization and prefabrication. The various parts of the building were premade in factories, cut to the right size, and packaged together. After the neighborhood's roads were built, the packages were dropped off at regular intervals, all along the roads. Workers operating digging equipment would move down the roads, digging the foundations. Behind them would come concrete workers, carpenters, plumbers, electricians, painters, and other construction workers. Each doing a few tasks on each house before moving on to the next house. This repetitive, factory approach to building allowed Levitt to use lots of machinery to speed up the work. This meant that each house took less work to make, and could be sold for less. Levitt built entire suburban communities with tens of thousands of houses at once—all identical and all selling at the same reasonable price.

There are various ways of combining financing, building, and developing, but large-scale house manufacturing like this has been the exception. Developers often have difficulty getting their hands on a large enough area of land to make the assembly line approach workable. And even when they can, they often choose to build small and quick, so that if the market takes a downturn they won't get stuck with houses they can't sell. Developing is often chaotic, done by individuals flipping houses. They buy a house or two in a hot neighborhood, do some minor (probably cosmetic) renovations, and sell them six months later for more money. Having good connections with local politicians and access to cheap loan money is very useful to developers, but the largest part of the profit from house building usually comes from land speculation. This is usually much larger than the surplus value created during the construction of the houses themselves. This means that there isn't much pressure to invent new ways to speed up the work process. Usually, the developer's main concern is promoting the most profitable land use and making sure the price of the land rises between the time they buy it and the time they sell it.

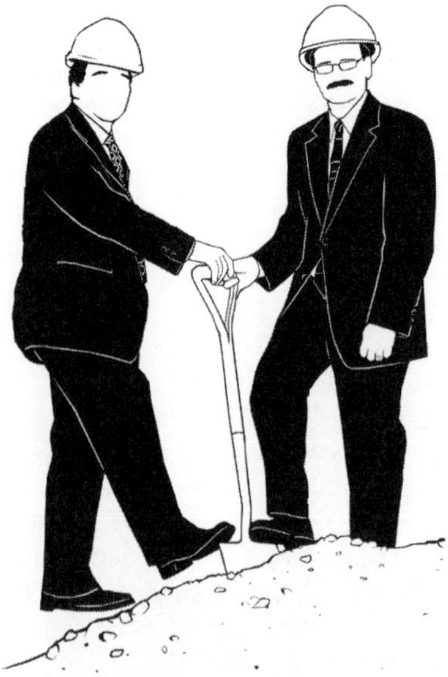

Housing development follows long-term shifts in the way industry and employment are organized. When shipping companies introduced standardized shipping containers, that could be moved from ships to trains to trucks and back, the number of people working on the waterfront fell drastically. A few crane operators replaced all the dock workers who used to board ships and carry and tie down cargo (in barrels, boxes, and sacks). The old working-class neighborhoods near the docks were broken up and replaced with warehouse districts or upscale waterfront tourist areas. At the same time, containerization also created some new trucking and warehouse jobs around the edges of the city, and many workers moved to the suburbs. Our houses have to be within reach of our jobs. Within the limits created by these long-term movements, developers take an active role in creating the housing market.

Developers will buy up property in a neighborhood that seems like its real estate could be used more profitably. One of the advantages of capital invested in the land is that new development doesn't usually have to destroy old investments. If an office invests in new, better computers, the investment in the old computers is lost. If an old brick building is fitted with fiber-optic cables so it can be rented out to a software company, the value of the building is still kept. Better yet, if the government spends money on the bus system, or on repaving roads, this makes it easier for people to get to a neighborhood. This costs the developer nothing, while raising the rent. Since infrastructure is expensive, and developers and landowners make a killing when they build new neighborhoods where there weren't any before,

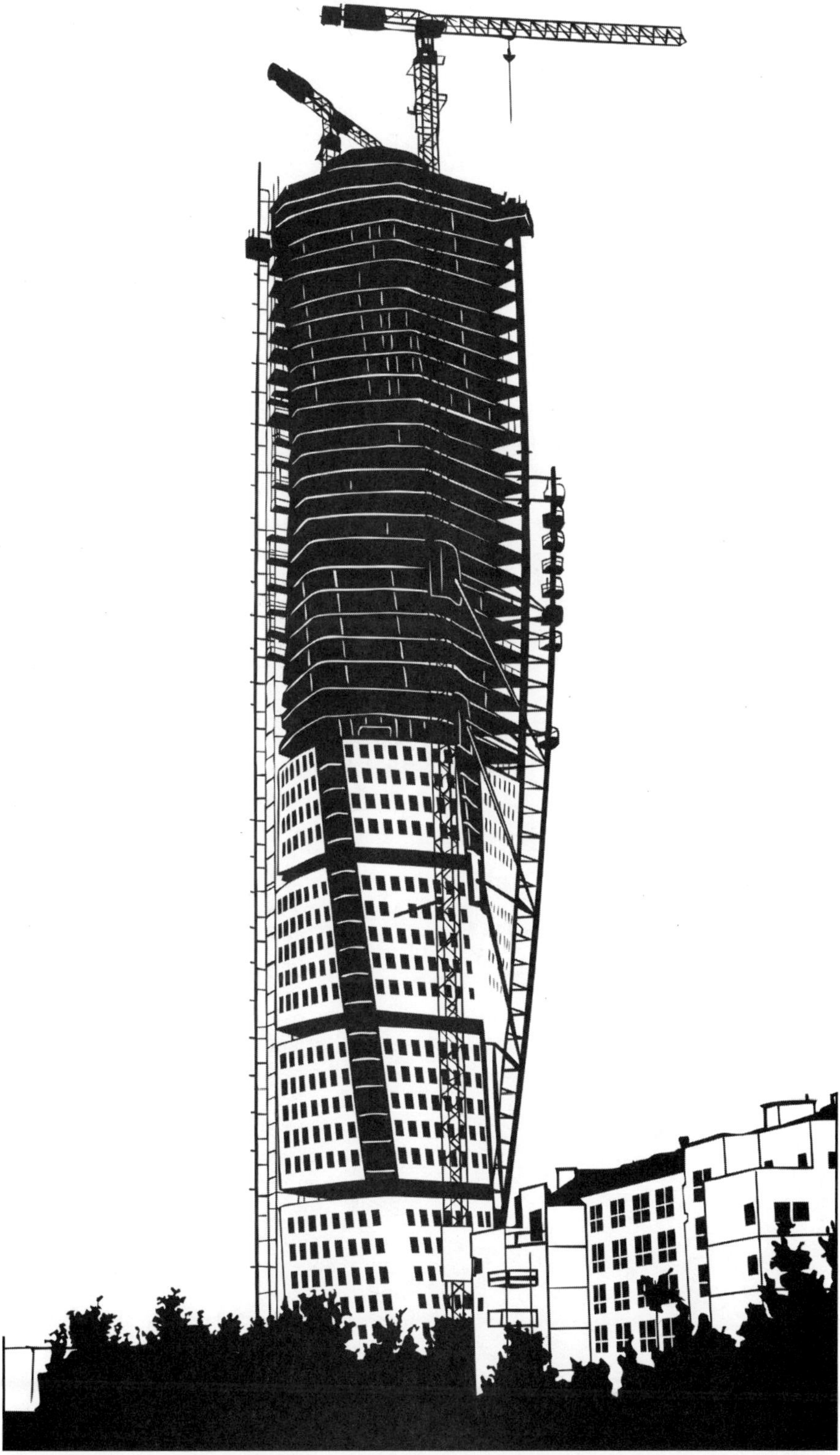

often governments will require them to pay for at least part of the cost of new roads, sewers, electric lines, and street lights, themselves. Just as often, development happens in already-existing neighborhoods. In this case, promoting the most profitable use of real estate often means turning neighborhoods with affordable housing, into neighborhoods for the wealthy—removing the inhabitants and replacing them with people who can pay higher rent. Development becomes a fight over a whole neighborhood.

In this fight, local government is the developers' most important ally. The city budget usually comes from property taxes, so increased property prices mean higher revenues for the city. As developers buy up land in a neighborhood, the city will raise the assessed value of the land in the rest of the neighborhood and increase property taxes accordingly. This

provides a push for other property owners in the neighborhood to switch to newer, higher-rent uses. The city's choices about how the transportation system is built can provide another push. Transit service between the developing neighborhood and the airport or downtown will be increased. A new highway will cut off the developing neighborhood from the slum next to it. And of course, there's the police. Aggressive patrols are increased and homeless people and panhandlers are beaten up and arrested.

Quick, speculative development is an obvious attack on us. The bars and cafés and corner stores we used to buy things at are replaced with more expensive versions of the same things. New luxury cars and an increased police presence are obvious. More importantly, rents go up. We have to work more to pay our rent or move to a new neighborhood and have a longer commute to work. Living in a neighborhood targeted by developers is eerie. You can almost feel how the built-in assumption in the land prices is that we will leave the neighborhood. This implied displacement creates resistance. We'll key a Porsche parked in an alley. We'll throw a brick through the window of a posh new restaurant. We'll glare at or harass the new luxury condo dwellers and try to make them feel as unwelcome as possible. We know they're just waiting for us to leave the neighborhood so they can label it a "renaissance."

Even when city planners and developers aren't actively trying to push up land prices, they can easily rise. As more people move to a city, as population grows, as more money is invested in the city's infrastructure, rents go up. These slow movements of the housing market are less dramatic, but have a similar effect. We're forced to work more to pay our rent or leave the neighborhood. A similar resentment toward new people moving into the neighborhood can be built up, but since it's a slower process, this resentment and fear have the effect of dividing working-class people against each other. Anti-gentrification sentiment can easily be completely reactionary. The unemployed and the underemployed resent those with steady jobs. The unskilled laborers resent those with more skills and higher pay. It can seem like they should just stay where they are—make different choices about where to live. But usually, the better paid workers have been pushed out of other neighborhoods by rising rents. The worker as consumer is as weak and pathetic as the worker as citizen.

A growing neighborhood is growing in opportunities for real estate investment. Community development and decay are the development or decay of profitability in a community. The surest way to stop neighborhood development is economic collapse. Imaginary capital in the land isn't different from imaginary capital in loans, and can be completely wiped out by a crisis. If a local economy goes into a full-on depression, no one is going to buy up property there and rents will fall. In a declining housing market, perfectly good houses won't be rented out because it's not profitable. Landlords will only be able to maintain their current rents by spending less on maintaining their buildings. Buildings will deteriorate. The city will spend less on maintaining the infrastructure. As the market bottoms out, the city will take over abandoned and tax-delinquent properties, and developers will buy up land for next to nothing and hold on to it. Banks will refuse to lend to anyone buying a house in the neighborhood. Drug and crime problems will get worse until the people left in the neighborhood are begging for some kind of rescue.

Then the developers can move in and start the "neighborhood recycling" all over again.

The decay and development of neighborhoods are both automatic market processes and the result of conscious action by developers and city planners. The same things that make us want to live in a neighborhood are what make it attractive to developers. Capital doesn't care if we feel at home somewhere. That feeling is a barrier to investment. It's an uncompetitive use of land to have cheap housing where you could have luxury hotels.

Housing investment grows and shrinks with the economy of the city, the country, and the world. The movements of capital shape our physical environment to its needs. Whether it's developing or decaying, the economy tends to do so at our expense.

The Housing Market and the Labor Market

"You can kill a man with an apartment as easily as with an axe."

Heinrich Zille

We sell our ability to work on the labor market. Assuming we're successful at finding a buyer, we go to work for a boss. Whether we work making things and providing services that the boss can sell, or speeding up the sale of the things the boss already owns, the things are the property of someone else. The capitalist makes money that he can live off and reinvest in the business. We get a wage, and we buy the things we need to survive. At the end of the day, we're in the same position. We're looking for a buyer of our ability to work, and the capitalist is looking to hire workers. The ability of the capitalist to use his property to make money implies a propertyless worker—it implies that we have no property we can make a living from and are therefore forced to sell our ability to work on the labor market.

For this social relation to keep replicating itself, we have to be paid enough money to keep showing up to work in a fit condition to work but not so much that our wages get in the way of our boss's profits. Still, the more he can force down our wages, the more profit he can make. Just as importantly, the more his competitors push down wages, the more pressure is put on him to force down wages. The more the work process can be divided up into simpler, repetitive tasks, the less skilled the worker. The less skill a job takes, the lower the wage—and the more people in competition for the job. The higher unemployment is, the more people in competition for jobs, the lower the wages.

We buy shelter on the housing market. Here, we deal with a different set of businessmen—landlords, real estate agents, and banks. They usually end up eating up a larger part of our wage than anything else. Housing, like everything else we need to survive, is a commodity. Unlike most other commodities, the right to use a house is bought slowly over a long period of time. If we lose our job or get our hours at work cut, we can easily stop going out to eat, or buy a cheaper brand of beer. We can't easily switch to a slightly smaller house or one slightly farther away. The need to keep up rent or mortgage payments is one of the main things keeping us going to work every day. The fact that landowners have the right to charge us money for a place to live, means that we have to keep selling ourselves on the labor market.

The price of housing includes the profit of construction companies, real estate agents, and landowners. They all have an interest in grabbing the largest part of our wage that they can. The more we pay in rent, the more money the landlord makes. The smaller apartment he can rent us for the same price, the more apartments he can rent out, the more money he can make. The fewer repairs he can get away with doing, the more money he can make. The fewer restrictions on eviction, the easier it is for him to rent his buildings out to the tenant who can pay the most rent at any given time. And the cost of land is further pushed up by the increased concentration of cities, new investment in infrastructure, and land speculation.

The tendency of the labor market is to push down wages. The tendency of the housing market to push up the cost of housing. This means that for all but the most skilled workers, a gap is opened up between the amount of

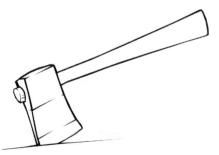

our wage we can afford to spend on housing and the price of housing. The result is that we end up living in houses that are overcrowded, dark, airless, damp, cold, moldy, dilapidated, and infested with rats, roaches, or bedbugs. All the charity and volunteerism of rich ladies, the moralizing about hygiene from scientific experts, or the new building designs from progressive architects

productive at work. This will cause problems for any business whose workforce is not made up entirely of day laborers. At a certain point, it's in the interest of business in general to put some restrictions on the business of renting out houses. And the state, as the representative of the needs of capital in general, will step in.

Still, an attack on the rights of one kind of property owner is easily

have not been able to get around the basic problem. The free market has never been able to provide decent housing for the vast majority of the working class.

But the slum solution to the housing problem can cause problems for business. If workers are losing sleep or getting sick because of overcrowded, unsanitary conditions, they will miss work or be less

interpreted as an attack on property in general. It took decades before governments in Europe and North America intervened in slum housing. The bourgeoisie was perfectly happy to let workers die of tuberculosis and rickets (called "tenement sickness" in Berlin), so long as they did so quietly in their slums, and kept having enough children to provide a growing workforce.

But the massive cholera outbreaks of the 1860s and 1870s did not stay isolated in the working-class neighborhoods. Cholera was in the water supply and killed both rich and poor. Fear of death pushed the bourgeoisie to overcome its fear of interfering with private property. In response to the epidemics, the first major housing laws were passed in many places as part of public health acts.

value of our wages and take the extra. Even if this doesn't get to the point of causing us to lose sleep, get sick, or die from bad housing, it still causes a problem for our employers. Employers are buyers on the labor market, and they have to compete, to some extent, with employers in other places for workers. If workers can get the same job for the same wage in two different cities, but in

The push and pull over housing is partially a struggle between employers and landowners. The landlord wants the boss to pay us a good wage which he can then take in the form of rent. Landlords find all sorts of ways of cheating us—like throwing in extra cleaning charges, security deposits, or demanding key money. By selling houses at a monopoly price, they lower the real

one city, the cost of housing is twice as much, companies there will have a much harder time attracting workers. They'll have to raise their wages based on the cost of living. And higher wages will make it harder to compete with the companies in the city with cheaper cost of living. Employers therefore have an interest in keeping housing costs under control.

Landowners and employers may fight each other through wages and housing costs, but this is only a fight over how surplus value is divided up. The landlord only wants our wages to go up, so he can charge us more in rent. The boss only wants housing costs to go down so he can pay us less wages. Both of them have an interest in us continuing to go to work and in keeping our standard of living as low as possible. The fight over real wages isn't just between workers and bosses. It's between the working class and the capitalist class (landowners included).

Capitalists have understood for a long time that inflation is as good a way of lowering wages as actually paying less money—especially if they're worried about provoking resistance. For us, it's just as bad to get decent pay and give most of it back in rent or mortgage payments, as it is to get shit pay and give most of it back in rent or mortgage payments. It's just as bad to have a sore throat from the mold or toxic insulation in the walls of our house as it is to have a sore throat from breathing in mold or toxic insulation at work. Our needs come into conflict with the needs of the capitalists we work for but also with the needs of the capitalist we buy housing from. The landlord wants to charge us more. We want to pay less. He wants to be able to evict us whenever he can find a more

profitable tenant. We want security of tenure. He wants to skimp on repairs and add in as many extra charges as he can. We want the house properly maintained and to not pay extra fees.

Capital's push to expand and to create the best conditions for further growth comes into conflict with our needs again and again. At work, at home, on public transportation, at school, at the grocery store, on the battlefield—class conflict can happen all over. But the different places that the conflict happen create different obstacles and opportunities. The workplace and the neighborhood are very different terrains.

In most workplaces, the work requires that workers cooperate. The work process itself brings us together. This can be a pain in the ass if we can't get along, but it is also the jumping-off point for us to fight against the boss. We might recognize the people who live in the same apartment building as us and trade hellos when we pass them in the street, but (except in the most overcrowded slum housing) there is no forced socialization. The natural tendency is separation and privacy—a tendency which is pushed to extremes in decentralized, ambulophobic, suburban neighborhoods.

At work, we're on the boss's time. He's pushing us, trying to get as much out of us as possible. Whatever our ideas about the world, the things

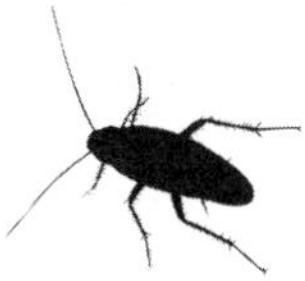

we do at work to keep from wearing ourselves out and driving ourselves crazy quickly bring us into conflict with the company's profitability. At home, we're on our own time. Time spent going door to door passing out flyers, or protesting against a landlord is less leisure time. And we're often too tired after work to do anything but have a beer and listen to some music (or maybe read an illustrated manifesto).

At almost every workplace people shit talk the company. As often as not this is just shit talking while we're hanging out before, after, or during work. Because neighborhood fights have to immediately break down the isolation of everyone going about their own private business, the initial communication, socialization, and community that is created is obviously linked to struggle. When we've gotten to the point of deliberately knocking on the doors of the other tenants in the apartment building we live in to see if the landlord is trying to screw them over the same way he's trying to screw us over, there's no mistaking it for idle shit talk. The very fact that housing organizing has to start off more deliberately can be an advantage.

Also the landlord has less power to break down this organizing before it starts. If we're standing around talking to our coworkers, the first response from the manager will be, "Get back to work!" Since housing organizing is done on our own time, this isn't a problem. And usually the landlord doesn't surveil us closely enough to see who's talking to who and stop it.

When we do take action together, when we're well organized and militant, we can change the balance of power. We can win wage increases while housing costs stay the same, or force landlords to provide better housing for the same price. We can raise the value of our labor and push up our standard of living.

But the basic working-class standard of living is constantly under threat. The definition varies over time and place, but whatever the definition, the combined action of the housing market and the labor market tend to erode it. Today's overpriced, dark, moldy, cockroach-infested basement apartments may well have microwaves and high-speed internet.

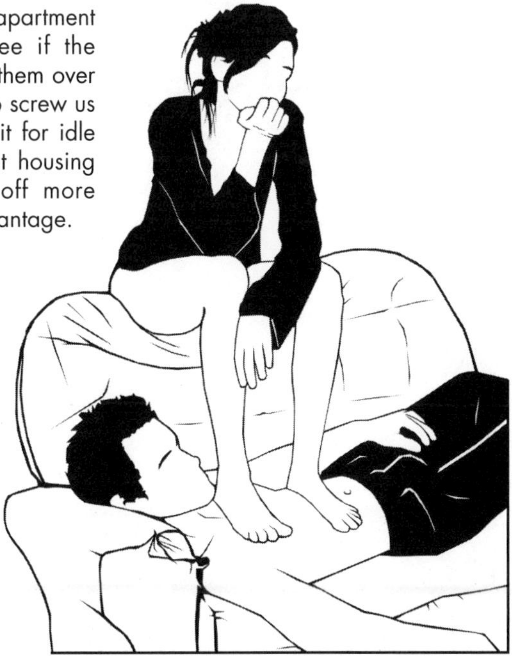

Ownership and Class

"No man who owns his own house and lot can be a communist."

William Levitt

It is most obvious that housing costs and wages are two parts of the same balance of power between classes when the landowner and the employer are the same person. Employers may provide housing for their workers because they're operating in remote areas, because they recruit employees from overseas on temporary contracts, because they want to keep housing costs under control, or because they want more control over their workforce. Whether the rent is taken out before or after we're given our pay, the relationship is clear, and the labor contract usually specifies both wages and rents.

Company housing is not in itself a solution to the problems caused by the way the housing market and the labor market interact. Either company housing is as overpriced as the housing available in the area anyway, or the company's housing business operates at an uncompetitive rate of profit—in which case the company's housing business is subsidizing its regular business. Often this is gotten around by only providing company housing for highly skilled workers, whose wages are high enough to afford decent housing anyway, and leaving the rest of the workforce at the mercy of the housing market.

Workers living in company housing (like workers dependent on company health care plans) are doubly tied to the company. If we quit our job or go on strike, not only will we not get paid, but we'll be evicted also. This lowers employee turnover and puts more pressure on the workers not to cause trouble. Companies sometimes actively use this double power to head off trouble, firing and evicting organizers, communists, or other potential troublemakers. Company housing has its advantages, but running a housing business alongside their regular business can be cumbersome. More often than not, employers don't bother providing housing for their workers.

When workers rent from a private landlord, the class relationship is the same, we just deal with two different capitalists. For the landlord, housing is his business and he wants to keep his business as profitable as possible. The landlord sees the house's value. What we see in the house is what it can be used for. We don't care what it's worth—we want shelter, privacy, a place to sleep and eat. If property values in the neighborhood go up, the landlord will raise the rent. As the landlord tries to make the most out of his investment, he enforces the movements of the housing market on us.

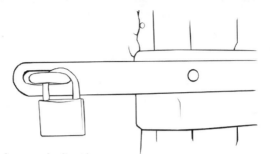

The landlord may deal with us directly or through some kind of property manager. A large property management company insulates the landlord from problems with his tenants but also takes a cut of his profits. Often landlords will give out one apartment in a building rent-free to a property manager whose job it is to collect rent and do repairs. In this case the property manager works part-time for the landlord and usually has another part-time job. She is in a contradictory position, probably struggling to survive, but also acting as the landlord's agent as he tries to get as much out of his investment as possible.

If small bosses are often worse than large ones, it's because large companies operate on a scale that allows them to use the most advanced machinery and produce efficiently, whereas small bosses have to make up for inefficiency by squeezing us harder. On the other hand small landlords are often better than large ones because they tend to want to minimize turnover more than they want to maximize rents. If they immediately raise the rent in response to changes in the housing market, they risk tenants leaving and having their apartments sit vacant for a month or two. The risk of vacancy compared to the benefit of increased rent is much higher for the landlord who rents out three or four apartments than for the landlord who rents out three or four hundred. Of course a smaller landlord will also be more likely to live nearby and to snoop around and spy on us at home.

In either case, for the worker who is also a tenant, we are almost as likely to get into a conflict with the landlord as with the boss. And it's no coincidence that the slumlord is a common demon in popular culture.

There is a wide spectrum of rental housing with varying amounts of security. The low end is usually for unskilled workers without regular jobs doing day labor, temp work, or living on welfare. Since the poorest sections of the working class can't afford to pay security deposits, and are seen as risky by landlords, they often have to pay rent weekly. These slum hotels are often in the worst condition, and workers living here often end up paying more in rent than workers with better, more secure housing. Extreme poverty is extremely profitable.

Even if landlords aren't worried about workers moving out in the middle of the night to avoid rent payments (because we've paid first and last months' rent already, for example), landlords will want to rent out to the least risky tenant. They may demand proof of employment, credit checks, or letters from previous landlords. Usually when we interview for an apartment we have to sound as middle-class as possible because we know we're subject to all the landlord's (rational and irrational) prejudices about what makes a good tenant. When a few people want to live together and split an apartment, we'll get the one person with a decent, respectable job to meet with the landlord and sign the lease.

In cities with strong tenants' rights laws that are enforced, renting can be somewhat more secure, and we might take some initiative to paint the walls or do other minor repairs or improvements ourselves. In places where tenants can be evicted at any time, for any reason, improving the apartment just feels like doing unpaid work for the landlord. Whatever the quality of rental housing, the house is someone else's property. Ownership of the land is ownership of the right to collect rent payments from the land. If they can't get the rent from us, we'll have to go. They'll either evict us, or just raise the rent and we'll be forced to leave. Rental housing is necessarily precarious. And tenants who plan to stay in the same place would usually rather buy than rent.

In a free market for home mortgages, only the highest-paid workers would be able to borrow money to buy homes. From the point of view of the banker, most working

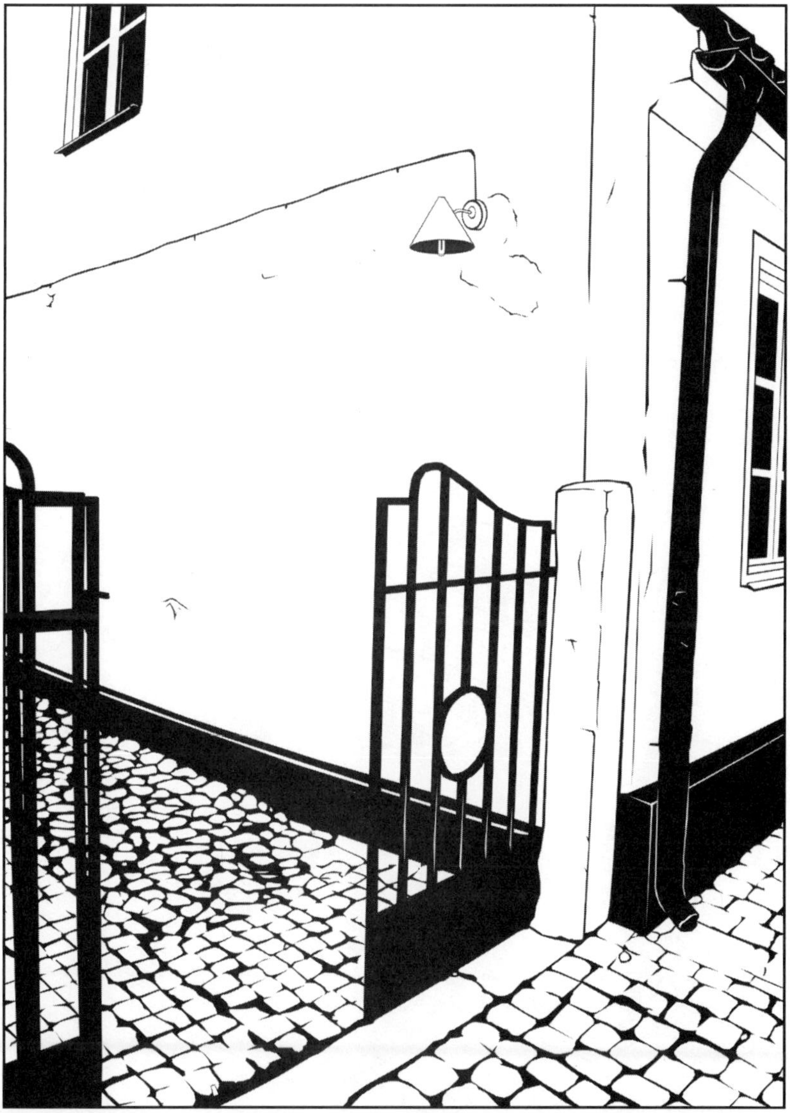

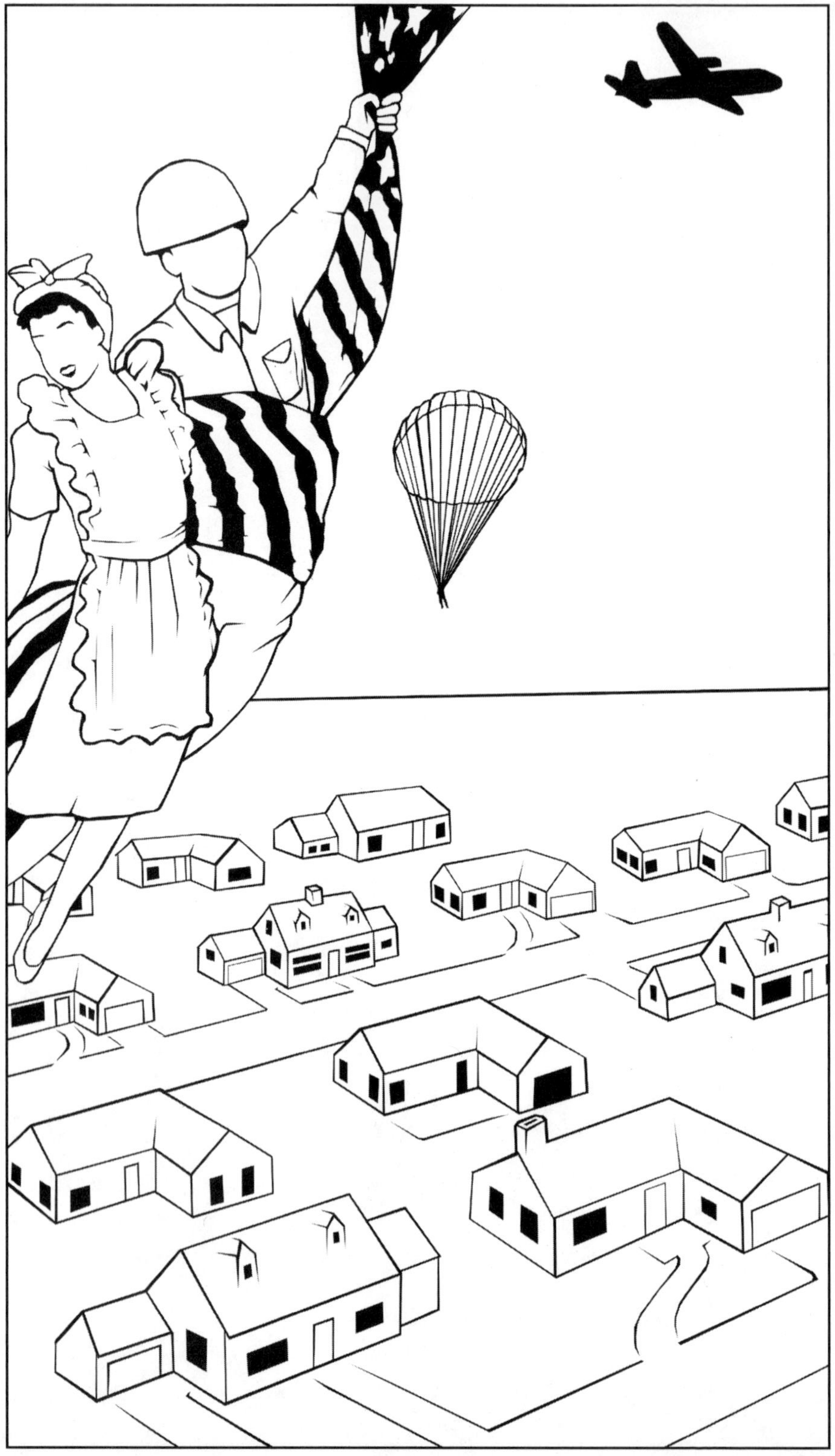

people are just too risky. Low wages mean small savings. We can't afford large down payments on houses and need large and fairly long-term loans. At the same time, we don't have any valuable assets that the bank could seize except the house itself. The only guarantee we'll pay off the loan is our job—and jobs are easily lost. For the loan to be worth the risk, the bank would have to charge an unaffordably high interest rate, and homeownership would be out of reach of most of the working class.

But there is rarely a free market in home loans. Governments spend huge amounts of money insuring home loans. This means the banks know they'll get their money back even if we can't pay them back. By pooling the risk and taking it on itself, this government insurance makes home loans much less risky for the banks. They are willing to lend at lower interest rates, with less money down, and for longer periods of time. One of the things that created the sustained demand for homes in the United States after the Second World War was that the US government's G.I. Bill provided veterans with loans to buy houses with no down payment necessary. On top of loan insurance, governments also give all sorts of tax breaks to homeowners. These various government subsidies can increase the quality of housing available to working people at the same time as they promote homeownership (as opposed to renting).

Homeownership is more than a question of whether we send monthly checks to the landlord or the banker. It is a cultural institution. The homeowner is supposed to be a recognized part of the neighborhood community and encouraged to participate in civil society. Even though the requirements that you own property in order to vote were dropped a long time ago, homeowners still vote and participate

in political parties at much higher rates than renters. Homeownership does not map neatly onto income, but working-class homeowners are usually the better-paid workers with steady jobs. It is sometimes possible for these workers to imagine themselves a respectable part of capitalist society. However subsidized their ability to buy a house, it seems like it was the product of their own hard work. Homeownership promotes individualism and is an important part of creating a middle class different from the rest of the working class.

Since homeowners own the land, the homeowner benefits from increased land values. Buying a home when we're in the prime of our working lives, waiting for the value to go up, then selling it and trading down to a smaller home once the kids have grown up has become, in some countries, the most important way working people ensure we have some money to live on during retirement. In this way, the working-class homeowner is forced to be a small land speculator. This ties us to the interests of capital accumulation. Homeowners may react very differently than tenants to development or decay in the neighborhood. The working-class homeowner can sometimes be mobilized behind the interests of landlords and developers in keeping immigrants and the poor (who might drive down property values) out of the neighborhood or in supporting police violence against the homeless to "clean up the streets" (and pave the way for rising property values).

Homeowners are contradictory. On the one had, we relate to the house as a place to live. Homeownership means that we can paint the house, remodel, build additions, upgrade. It means there's no landlord snooping around looking for an excuse to evict us so he can turn the place into condos and rent it out for more money. On the other hand, we relate to the house as an investment. We need to keep it in good shape so it can be resold for more money when land prices go up. This contradiction isn't a choice. By living in the house, we relate to it as something useful. By owning it, we relate to it as an amount of value—and property taxes put pressure on the homeowner to make the most profitable use of their property. Homeownership is not a way to escape from the landlord and the housing market. It just means that we become our own landlord and have to watch the housing market ourselves.

Sometimes homeowners will take in a lodger to help pay the mortgage. This is usually not much different from the tenants sharing an apartment who get only the most respectable one of them to sign the lease. At the point where the homeowner starts treating their property as a business, living off the rent, cramming in the lodgers and charging them as much as possible, they become a small, live-in landlord.

Homeownership is not an escape from working-class life. It is a way of controlling working people and pitting us against each other. Government and business support

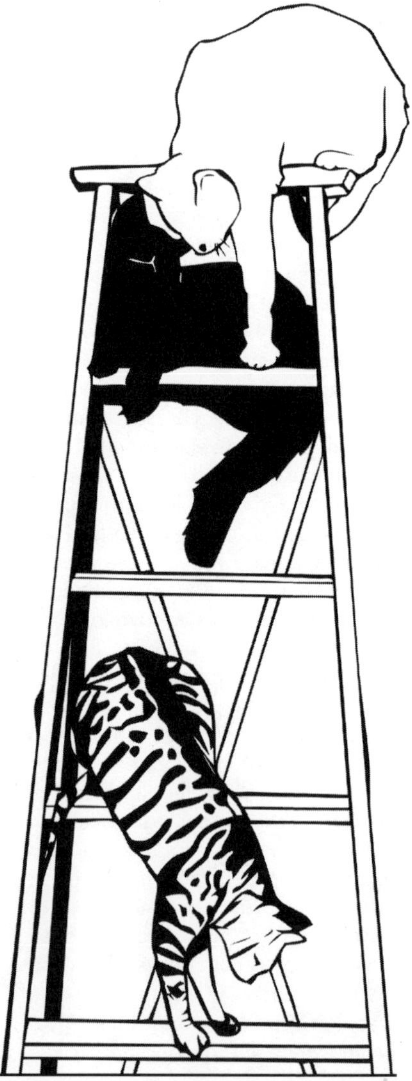

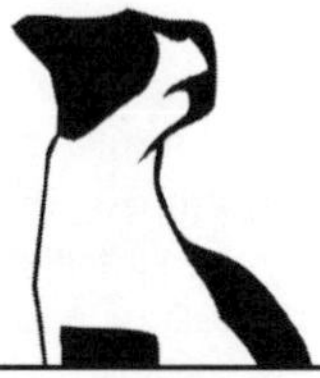

it for this reason. If we own a home somewhere, we are at the mercy of the local job market. We can't easily move to another city with higher wages. When Elbert Gary, the chairmen of US Steel Corporation, founded Gary, Indiana, as a site for a new steel mill, the company sold their skilled workers houses at below market prices with deals on mortgages. This was explicitly justified as a way to keep workers from leaving town, to keep them tied to the company and to keep them from causing trouble.

While the homeowner has more security than the tenant, other aspects of their housing situation may be just as bad. In rural areas, even the very poor often own their own houses, shacks, or trailers. Whether renting or owning, working-class houses will be the ones that were built on a landfill, or are downwind of the refinery or the chemical plant. Working all the time and struggling to pay the mortgage is no better than working all the time and struggling to pay the rent. And not paying the mortgage will lead to foreclosure, just like not paying the rent will lead to eviction. In times of rapidly rising land prices, the homeowner may see individual investment in property as a better way to advance their interests than collective class action. Still rapidly rising land prices can mean rapidly rising property taxes, which put pressure on the homeowner to sell the land and move somewhere else, so it can be used in a more profitable way. When the speculative bubble pops, it can wipe out not only the homeowner's savings, but also their image of themselves as middle-class.

On the one side, homeownership mixed with skilled jobs can create a middle class separate from the rest of the working class. On the other side, slum housing, projects, and homelessness mixed with immigration and racism can create a separate underclass. To be homeless is more than not to have a house—it is to be excluded, barely a member of capitalist society, a derelict, a vagrant, a bum. It's hard to find a job or get an unemployment check without a fixed address. It means living outside, sleeping on park benches and alleys, and constantly being harassed by the police.

Homelessness, like unemployment, is not a malfunctioning of the system. It's how the system works. On the one hand, it's a simple matter of supply and demand—houses are not rented to people who don't have enough money to pay for them. More importantly, the presence of homelessness is a constant reminder to the rest of the working class that we could be even worse off.

Unless the balance of power has shifted quite a bit in our favor, government housing is specifically designed not to interfere with this function of extreme poverty. Shelters have curfews, restrictive rules, and very little privacy. Government rent subsidies are quickly taken away if the landlord complains about the tenant. Public housing is falling apart and sometimes unsafe. Like the 19th-century poorhouse, the point is to be miserable, humiliating, demeaning, not to alleviate suffering. In this respect, the professional social workers who publicize the misery of the poor (like the activists who constantly complain about how security cameras are everywhere)

do as much to further social control as they do to make things better. A system of public housing that provides decent houses and is easily available to those that need it is a malfunctioning public housing system.

Houses sit empty, and land is not used to build houses because it's not profitable to do so. At the same time there are people without houses and people living in overcrowded houses. The legal right to use a house as shelter is not given because it can't be brought together with the legal right to make a profit off shelter. In this situation, one obvious response is to break the law—squatting.

We'll break into abandoned buildings, fix them up, do illegal water and electricity hookups. The landowner's natural response is to call in the police to evict us and reestablish the link between the use and profitability of the house. If they don't find out we're there, or if there doesn't seem to be any possibility of the house turning a profit any time soon, the landlord may not go to the trouble to get us kicked out, and we can live in squatted housing for a long time. Especially on government land, when there is political pressure on the government, squatting can become secure enough that people build houses themselves on squatted land. Tolerating widespread squatting is essentially a social housing program used by governments from Mumbai and Manila to Mexico City, from Cairo and Cape Town to Caracas—an indirect social housing program that can be taken away at any time.

It's not just government force that makes it so that land and houses can only be used if they make a profit. Houses are commodities, have value, are bought, sold, rented, exchanged, are part of the economy. The government keeps the peace, arbitrates, defends property, guarantees contracts, and backs up the economy. But the economy is an expression of the alienated social relations between people. When a squatter settlement stays around long enough, and it seems that the government, who formally owns the land, won't enforce its ownership any time soon, the people on the land are likely to start acting like owners. Houses will be bought and sold. Rental housing will reappear. A black market in housing will develop. The titles to ownership on the black market are not legally backed up by the state. They require some kind of semi-state or sub-state to back them up and to keep the peace. Gangs, mafias, militias, political parties, brotherhoods, religious movements, may take over this role. Class and ownership are not legal questions.

In the late 19th-century company town, the skilled workers got loans from the company to buy houses built by the company. The unskilled workers lived just outside of town and rented slum housing from private landlords or lived in tents or shacks. They both worked for the company doing different jobs. Division of labor at work and different housing situations reinforced each other and created divisions among the workers.

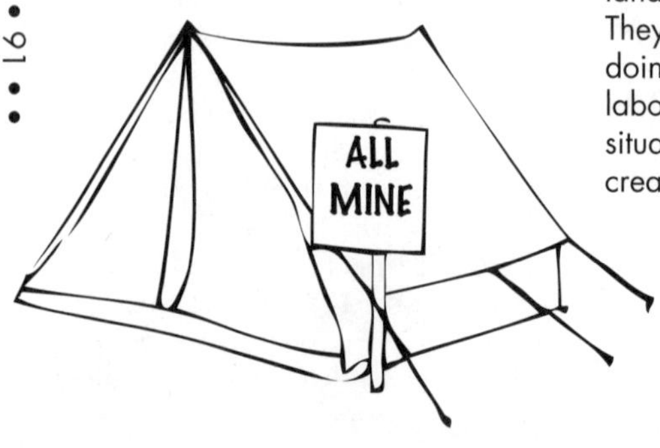
ALL
MINE

Both workers walked to work on roads built by the company, went to churches funded by the company, went to see the company doctor, bought food at the company store, took out books from the library owned by the company, saw shows put on by the company's theater, read newspapers funded by the company's money, giving the company's point of view, and if they went on strike they were both beaten up or shot by the company's private police.

Today the worker who gets yelled at by the foreman and is struggling to make his mortgage payments almost always has a different boss from the worker who gets yelled at by customers and is struggling to pay her rent. Divisions in the labor market and the housing market still reenforce each other. There may be many different businesses selling us a variety of ways to get our news, our food, our transportation to work, our religion, our entertainment. But the two sides of the class relationship that capitalist society grows out of are the same today as they were in the 19th century. Every town is a company town.

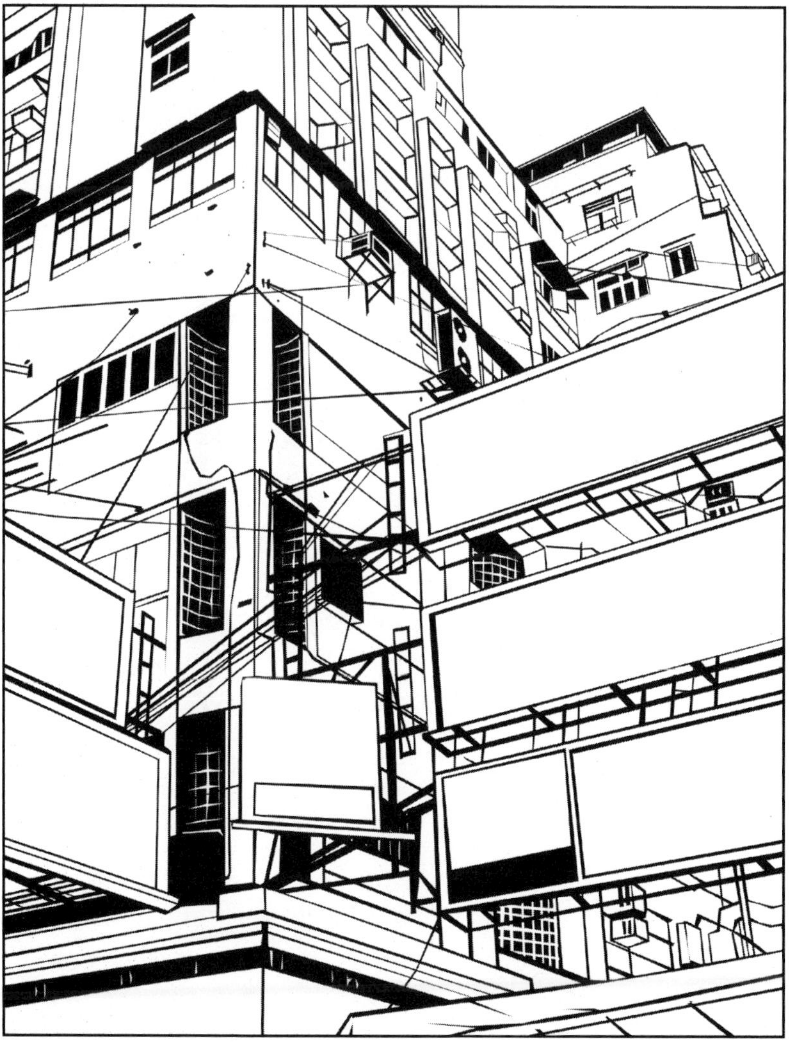

A Woman's Place

"I am a marvelous housekeeper.
Every time I leave a man I keep his house."

Zsa Zsa Gabor

Not all relations in a capitalist society are value relations. The construction and sale of commodities presupposes and interacts with relationships that have very little to do with production for exchange. The economy develops on top of these relationships, creates the context in which they develop and puts pressure on them to develop in certain ways. The house is a central place where these two kinds of relationships come together.

In Medieval Europe, the household was a very different thing than it is today. Most people were small peasant farmers, who lived on or near the land they farmed and produced most of what they needed at home. The craftsmen in the cities would usually live above their workshops. Apprentices lived with journeymen or both lived as part of the household of master craftsmen. And aristocratic households were even larger. They were based around a noble family but included as members of the household cooks, laundry women, stable hands, maids, and a number of other live-in servants. There was a market, money lending, merchants, and labor was even sometimes done in exchange for a wage. But production had not been taken over by the market, and turned into production for exchange. The basic production unit of society was the household. Home and work were usually the same place.

Medieval Europe was patriarchal. Male heads of households were in charge, and women had very

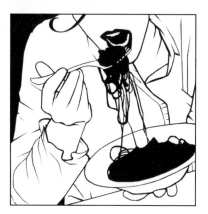

limited property, inheritance, and other legal rights. Still, because production was centered in the household, women participated in productive activity. Aristocratic women were usually under the control of their husbands and fathers, sometimes married away for political purposes, but they also had a central role in managing the household and the servants. Wives and daughters of craftsmen were usually excluded from guilds, but it was assumed that they would take part in the trade practiced in their household (and sometimes wives took over the running of the trade if the husband died). Peasant women may not have done the hard labor in the fields, but they picked up the extra tasks that needed to be done—taking care of the vegetable or herb garden and the poultry, shearing the sheep, milking the cow or the goat, making butter, cheese, or bread, brewing ale, making and mending clothes, and taking anything extra to market. Women's work filled in and backed up the productive activity in the household.

As the capitalist mode of production developed, all this changed. Things were increasingly made outside the home. Instead of peasant women using spinning wheels at home, or weavers using hand looms in the home-workshop, the

process of making cloth was broken down into its different parts, each done by different weaving workers in a factory using mechanical looms—water powered, then steam powered. Production became more and more production for the growing market—production of value. The traditional class relations between peasants or servants and their lords, between apprentices, journeymen, and master

company housing was one response to this. By buying up land around the factory and housing the workers there, workers could spend more time working and less time walking to work. As state-subsidized mass transit systems were created, streetcars and subways moved wage workers quickly from home to work and back. This reduced the need for employer housing and increased the distance

craftsmen were eroded as the market expanded. Productive activity was increasingly disentangled from other activities and the ability to work became everywhere a commodity. A new class relationship was created—the relationship between wage workers and capitalists. Wherever it was imposed, capitalism created these same relationships. Work separated itself from the rest of life in time and space. The people you ate dinner with were no longer the people you worked with, and the two were done in increasingly distant places.

By separating the workplace from the home, capitalism invented the commute. As property prices in newly industrialized cities climbed, workers were forced to walk further and further to get to work. Early

between home and work. The mass-production of the private automobile pushed this even further.

For thousands of years, women in Western civilization had not had an equal place in society to men. A woman's place was in the home. So long as the basic units of production in society were households, though, women participated in production, and inequality was somewhat lessened. As more and more things were manufactured outside the home, the capitalist firm replaced the household as the basic unit of production. The household was hollowed out. A strict dividing line between work and housework developed and a new capitalist household began to form. To the extent that women were stuck at home and did not participate in wage labor or the running of businesses, they were increasingly isolated, unequal, and cut off from public life.

The capitalist household is a unit of consumption. Commodities that are produced and bought elsewhere are taken home to be consumed together as a household. And the house itself is a commodity that is collectively consumed by

Capitalism creates divisions between mental and manual work, between skilled and unskilled work, between agricultural, manufacturing, and service work, between work and unwaged activities. These divisions of labor interact with all the other differences already existing in society, and different jobs get associated with different kinds of people, based on their sex, ethnicity,

the household. Housework may be individual, lonely, hard, tiring, but it is also direct. When meals are cooked for the family, they get from the people who make them to the people who need them without having to be exchanged. They have no value. Cooking, cleaning, washing, doing the laundry, are done for what they produce, not in order to create surplus value and profit. Serving a meal to house guests is like serving food to customers in a restaurant in only the most superficial way—the same way that knitting a pair of socks for a family member is like working in a sock factory operating computerized circular knitting machines. Housework is, by definition, unproductive under capitalism. It does not produce value, and no one profits off it.

immigration status, etc. This creates attitudes of superiority and fear or resentment and anger dividing working people against each other. To the extent that being a woman means staying at home and being a specialist in unpaid activity, the rift between home and work is the basis for inequality. As more and more activities leave the household, being isolated in the house becomes more and more crippling and oppressive.

Like many of the ideals that circulate in capitalist society, "traditional" family values are constantly undermined by the circulation of value. Under capitalism, family life is expensive. The more children a common medieval family had, the more farm hands or apprentices there were to help out. A wage worker can't bring his children to work with him to cut down on the amount of work he has to do. To the modern worker, children and housewives are extra mouths to feed. The guys working three jobs and always looking for overtime are inevitably the ones with big families. Supporting a full-time housewife is a bit of a luxury, and the further down the income scale, the less possible it becomes. Low wages and long work hours can easily cause family life to disintegrate. And the poorest, homeless parents can sometimes have their children taken away by government social services on economic grounds alone. "Traditional" family values perpetuate inequality, but they are popular exactly because they are constantly under attack by capital.

The authority of the head of the household is no longer essential to the system. Now it's workers at work who need to be controlled. The rich woman and the poor women both may suffer from isolation and exclusion, but there is no sisterhood. Working-class women have always had to work—often at low wage jobs and often dealing with the housework after work. For the rich, housework can be dumped on the hired help. What improves the situation of working women and the situation of businesswomen are not the same things. Only the most narrow-minded feminist could imagine that increasing the number of female CEOs and politicians is somehow a gain for working women. Having limited options to participate in exploitation is a completely different exclusion from being exploited for low pay.

Margaret Thatcher was not a step forward for the working women of England.

The market has to keep expanding. Direct relationships have to be commodified. The housewife who used to bake bread, more likely buys it from a bakery. More expensive canned beans replace dried beans that need to be cooked for hours. With restaurants, cooking is moved completely out of the house. What used to be housework is now someone's job. Productive work is work that creates surplus value for a boss—and there is constant pressure to make everything productive. People aren't born and don't die at home anymore except by accident. No one but eccentric hippies and religious fundamentalists educates their children at home anymore. The cases where work reenters the house, it is an invasion. The woman who assembles plastic toys at home for a piece wage while she watches her children, or the internet sex worker who sets up a camera in her bedroom are not doing housework.

To oppose value relationships from the point of view of the wholesome household is incoherent. The privacy, intimacy, and isolation of the household only exist in contrast to the public, impersonal contact of the market. When we begin to fight for our class interests, we come into conflict with both worlds.

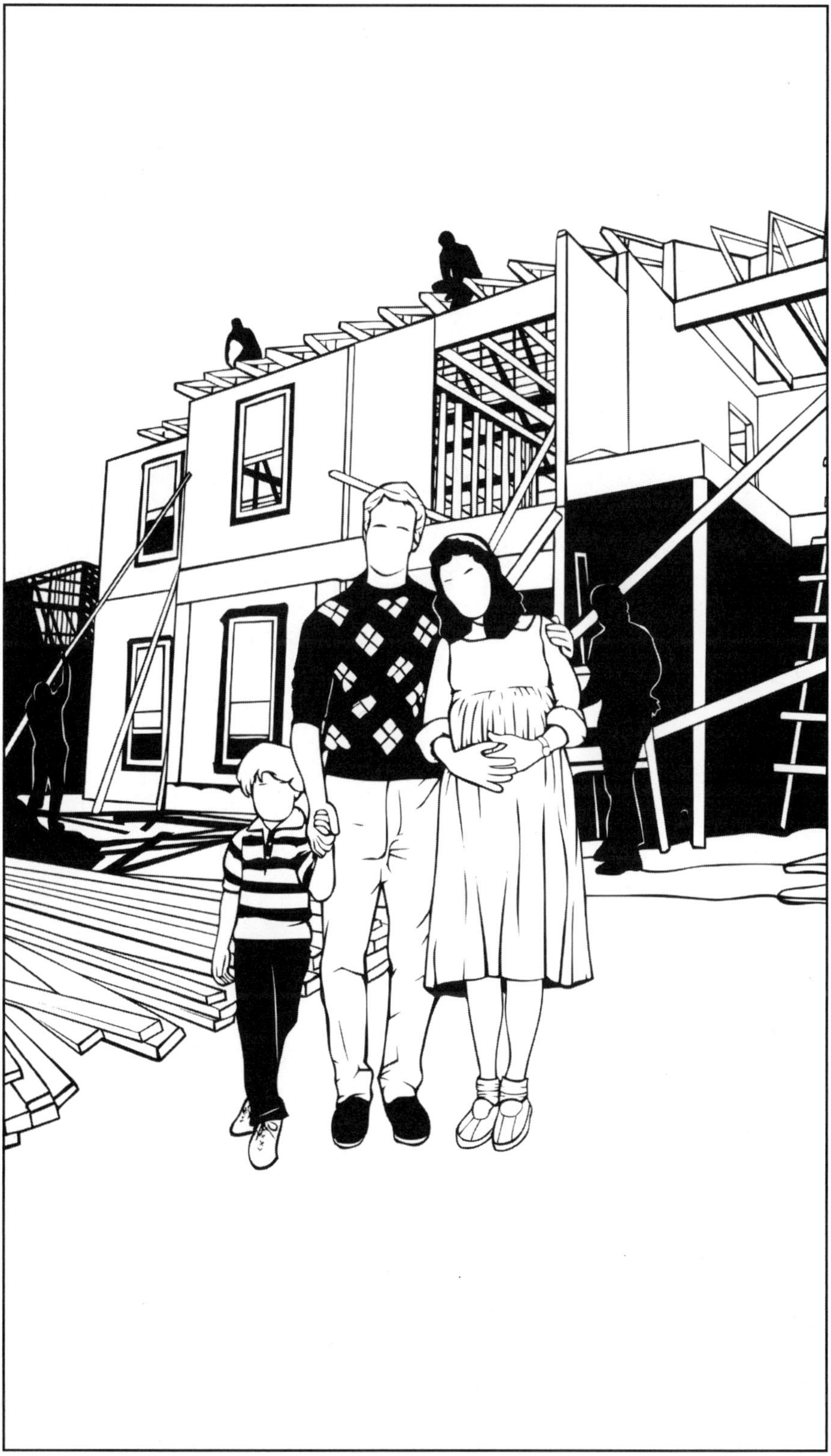

Community and Commodity

"Basically, I'm for anything that gets you through the night—
be it prayer, tranquilizers, or a bottle of Jack Daniels."

Frank Sinatra

When we walk—or even drive—around a neighborhood we get a certain feel for it. The varying widths of the streets, the sidewalk traffic, the screech of elevated transit, the kinds of trees, buildings, and from the people we live next door to, pass in the street, or drive by, as from people living on the other side of the planet.

We do come into contact with people in the neighborhood every

cars, the styles of clothing people are wearing, the shops, restaurants, cafés, the weather, the billboards, the graffiti, the wheat-pasted posters, the languages spoken, the look on people's faces as you pass them on the street, the smell of the bakery mixed with gasoline fumes, the music from passing cars or buskers— all these crystallize together in an idea of the neighborhood's identity. Where we live can be as important in how we think of ourselves as what kind of work we do.

But living near each other does not make a community. Unless there is some kind of direct relationship, we will be as isolated day, but it's on the market. We exchange hellos at the same time that we exchange money for commodities. The relationship only happens as a footnote to the act of exchange. Most of what we do is work. And the work of different people is connected only through the exchange of commodities. The specific activities we're doing at work lose most of their meaning and become just work that helps our boss's capital to expand itself. It's completely transparent that the girl working in the corporate coffee shop is enthusiastically interested in how our day is going because it's company policy. But even the regular,

friendly conversations we have with the guy working at the deli counter at the local grocery store would be interrupted if the grocery store a few blocks further away started selling their cheese cheaper.

As more and more activities move out of the house, they become commodities. More and more of our contact with people is through commodity exchange. We talk to them while they're working and we're buying something (or the other way around). For the person working at a store, the contact with customers is part of the job—a way to make money to survive, not interesting in itself. For the customer, the store is a place to buy the things they need. The tendency of commodity exchange is toward separation, fragmentation, isolation, loneliness.

This destruction of community affects both the rich and the poor. The difference is that the rich sometimes think they can buy their way out of it. They'll mistake the waitress's flirting for something other than an attempt to up her tip. They'll think a bartender or a cleaning lady who's talking to

them is their friend. They'll buy a lap dance in a private room in the back of a strip club and end up just hugging the stripper and crying. The centrifugal force of market society is terrible and creates an intense desire for some kind of community.

And any intense desire is a good marketing opportunity. Everything is called "a community" today—"the black community," "the immigrant community," "the gay community," "the disabled community," "the financial community," "the fair trade coffee community," "the anarchist community." It doesn't matter that the people making up the community likely have no relationships with each other whatsoever. Since capital can't create real community, it creates imaginary ones. But being part of an imaginary community doesn't make someone any less isolated. The need for some kind of community is still there.

This is the real basis of religion under capitalism. No one ever found the Lord because they were convinced by rational argument that evolution is wrong and the earth is only 6,000 years old. The purely rationalist

critique of religion is inevitably elitist, because religion is about community, not rationality. Isolated at home and brought together under the control of the boss, activities at the church, the mosque, the temple are a chance to be part of a larger community. From the backwoods of Appalachia to the suburbs of Beirut, religious organizations organize direct social relationships outside of work. These communities are controlled by religious leaders but are very different from the dictatorship at work. It's exactly because market forces constantly undermine and attack direct social relationships that religion is so popular.

The people who go to a local church have direct relationships with each other. So do the people who meet regularly in the park to play football or chess. The image of a neighborhood community is built on top of these real relationships. It grows out of the neighborhood's real history, architecture, feel, but as it becomes officially recognized, it becomes a stereotype of itself and imposes itself back on the community.

The image of the neighborhood can then be mobilized (by the left or the right) against anyone new moving into the neighborhood, who might not take part in the existing communities (and therefore undermine the authority of the traditional community leaders). Gentrification can be blamed on gay people in San Francisco, white people in Philadelphia, and anglophones in Montreal. Falling property values can be blamed on black people, immigrants and people living in

public housing. This is effective in getting us fighting each other, but not very effective in keeping the character of a neighborhood from changing.

A neighborhood can only continue to exist in a particular form, because of the interactions between the housing market, the job market, the local government's development plans, and the movements of capital on financial markets. If there is a change in any of these and a different potential use for a neighborhood becomes more profitable, or the current use of the neighborhood becomes unprofitable, the neighborhood will begin to develop or decay. It may keep its image of itself, but its reality has to change.

At a certain point, the image of the neighborhood community becomes just a blurb on propaganda aimed at tourists. Real, authentic, traditional communities are a valuable commodity, but by being organized for sale they lose their reality and authenticity.

The real control that religious and other community leaders have over their communities, backs up and gives reality to the imaginary neighborhood community. Successful

city politicians build their careers by having relationships with the community leaders in each neighborhood. Every neighborhood, like every country, is a mixture of conflicting interests. The people who work at the local café don't have the same interests as the café owner. The people who go to the local church soup kitchen don't have the same interests as the politicians who fund it. When we start to stand up for our interests, we quickly come into conflict with the leaders of most of the real and the imaginary communities that exist in the neighborhood.

Capital, whether invested in the construction of houses or some other commodity, needs to move and expand. The general contractor, the subcontractor, the developer, the banker, the investor, the landlord, the corner store owner, the café owner, all need to make as much profit out of their business as they can. This means squeezing us, exploiting us, cheating us, eating up as much of our time as possible. Dead labor needs to keep accumulating, and it can only do so at our expense.

That's just the way things are.

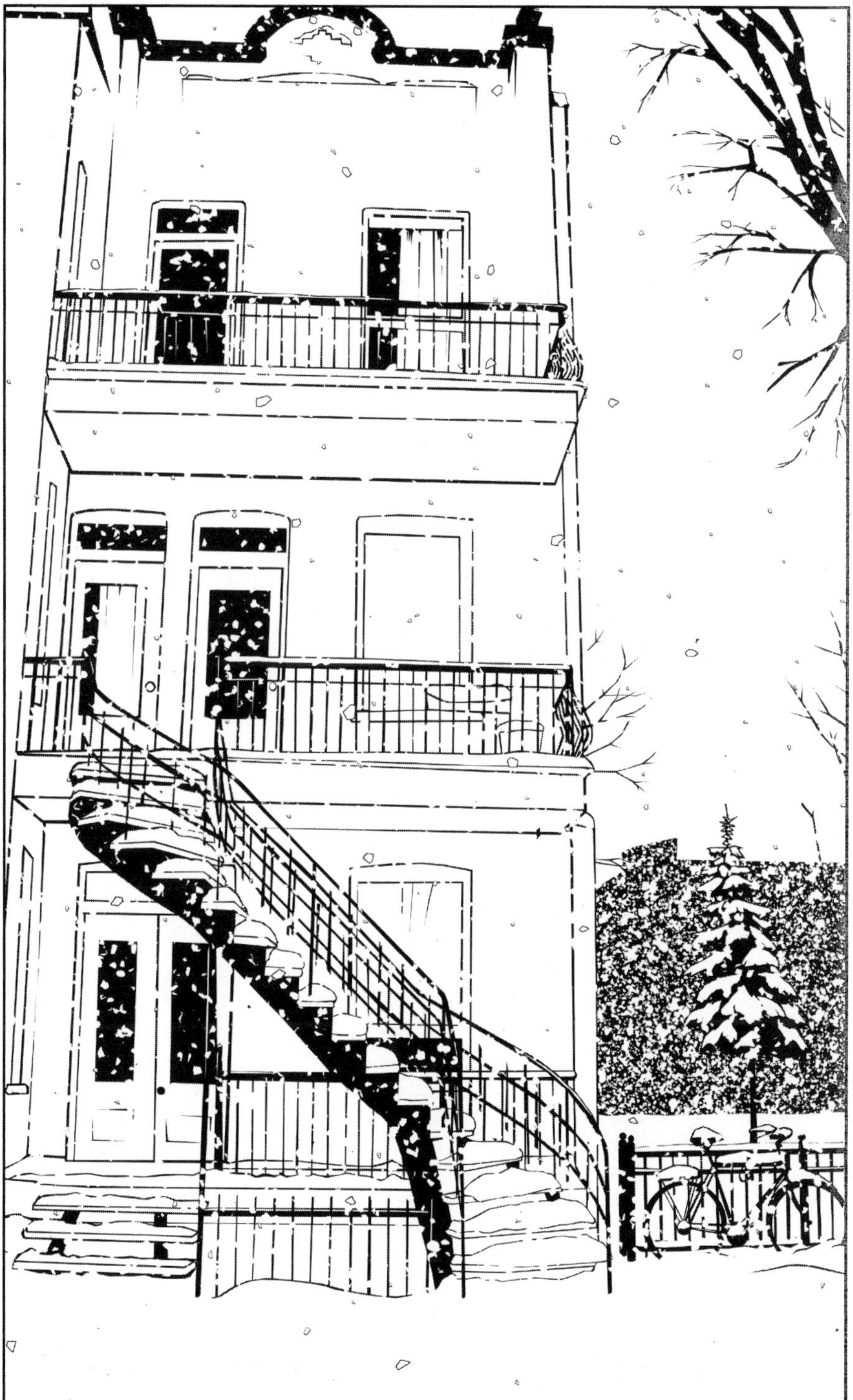

PUSHING, PULLING, AND BREAKING

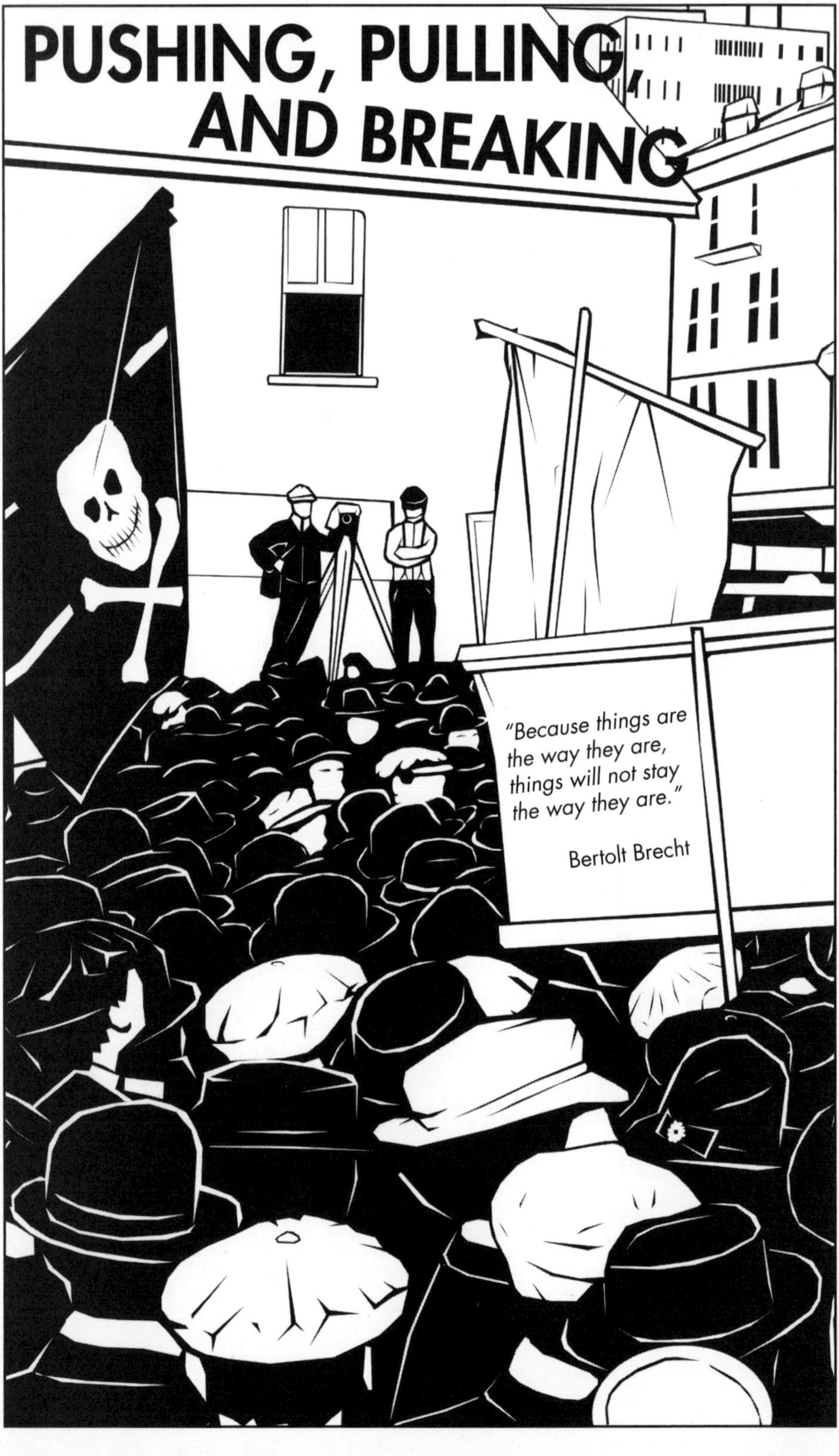
"Because things are
the way they are,
things will not stay
the way they are."
Bertolt Brecht

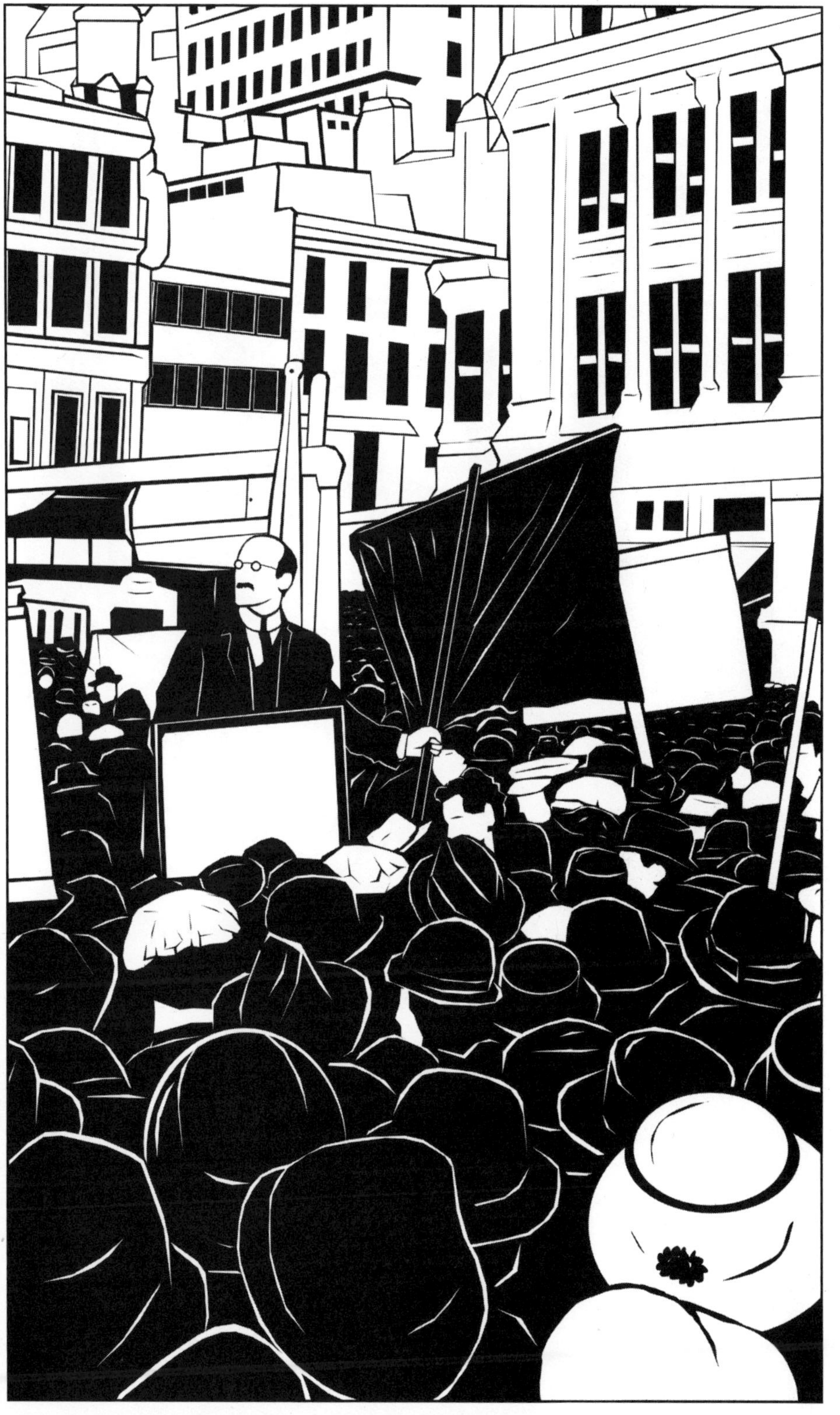

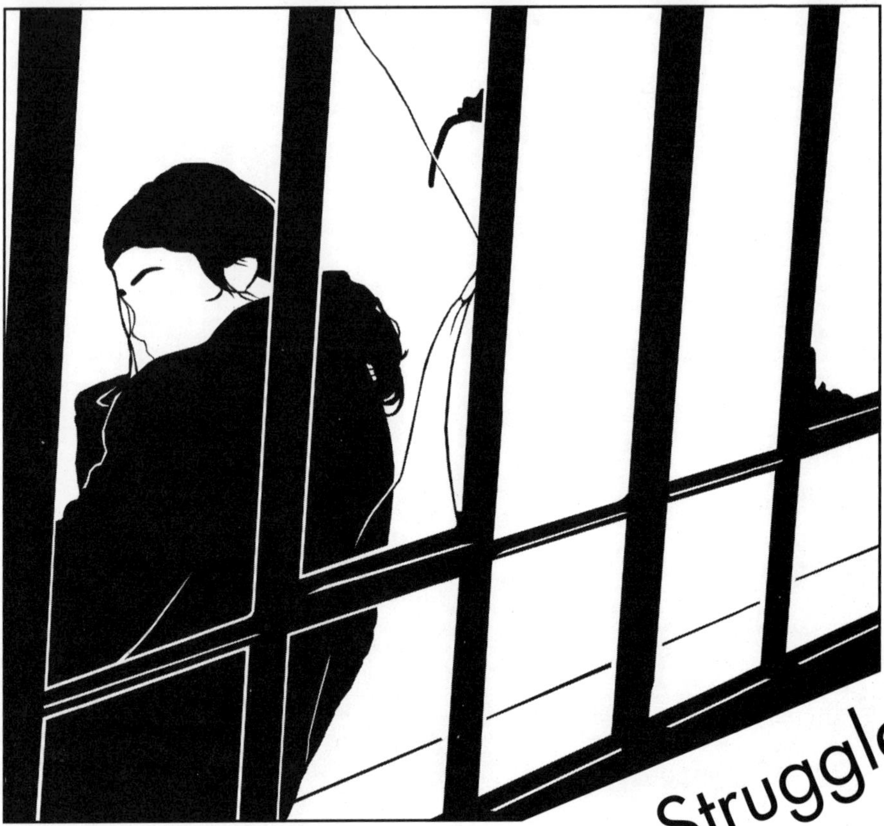

Notes on the Class Struggle

"I can be influenced by what seems to me to be justice and good sense; but the class war will find me on the side of the educated bourgeoisie."

John Maynard Keynes

But a situation of zero struggle is impossible under capitalism. Capital has to grow or die. Businesses have to be profitable and competitive. They have to push us to work harder, for less. They have to attack our standard of living. Everything has to be shaped and reshaped to the needs of capital accumulation, or the economy stagnates. Capital is constantly looking for new and better ways to squeeze us.

Our everyday lives are a struggle—to survive, to make work as painless as possible, to keep capital from eating up every day of our lives.

When we start to fight for our own interests, a contrast is quickly visible—a contrast between our needs and the needs of capital accumulation. This contrast is what class and class struggle are all about.

As we struggle to survive, we see that other people around us are in the same position. We work together to fight for ourselves. As our needs come into conflict with the needs of capital accumulation, we come into conflict with the people who benefit from capital accumulation: capitalists. As class struggle develops, deepens, intensifies, it becomes clearer who's on our side.

Some of the guys working for a small construction company might have talked to the boss and thought he was a nice guy, but the friendly atmosphere quickly disappears when the boss starts to put pressure on the guys to work faster. When there's a strike or conflict, the manager, foreman, or supervisor who's paid only a little more than the rest of the employees is forced to choose a side. Taxi drivers, truck drivers, or nurses who are classified as "independent contractors" go on strike. The police officer who we might have had a friendly conversation with at the bar is called in to evict squatters, to shoot rioters, or to break up the illegal picket lines of striking workers. The underlying class relationship

T he worker who gets a bad back from heavy lifting and the worker who gets a bad back from sitting in the same chair all day do not necessarily identify with each other. The worker who can't travel because she's working all the time and the worker who can't travel because she has no job and therefore no money to travel can feel like they have very different problems.

Where class struggle is not obvious, class itself can seem like a strange concept. Everyone can seem like an individual commodity seller trading on the market, or a citizen with equal rights in a political process. The only way to change anything seems to be making exchange more equal and extending political rights further. The real social relationships at the base of society are invisible, taken for granted, misunderstood, or just unnecessary.

From the point of view of an advertising firm or a politician trying to get a message across, there's no need to look at these social relationships. Society is chopped up into demographic slices based on political preferences or purchasing power. A sociolinguist studying how speech patterns relate to income might look at society and find six or seven or eight classes.

SOCIAL PEACE

be a top-down move by a union bureaucracy meant to head off any expression of that power. A squat can be a direct confrontation of our needs and the needs of capital invested in the land. It can also be a marginalized and irrelevant adventure for strange-looking kids. A "defeat" can be demoralizing and destroy a movement, but it can also lead to regrouping, widening, and strengthening of a movement. A "victory" can drive the struggle forward, but it can also mean institutionalization and dissipation of the movement. What counts as a real gain and a loss is not always immediately obvious.

Whenever we start to fight for our interests there is immediate pressure to look at things from the perspective of capital and to make demands that don't cause any problems.

Sometimes we'll make demands that are weak, divisive, or self-defeating all on our own—demands for stricter immigration controls or more barriers to entry into a job, demands for more differentiation in the workforce based on education,

becomes more clear. It becomes less and less of a simplification to see society as divided between those with loaded guns, and those who dig.

Quietly working or apart in our apartments, it's impossible not to feel alone, weak, and powerless. As we come together and fight for our interests, a different kind of community is formed. Prejudices are weakened or broken down. Class conflict comes out of the basic capitalist social relationships, but when it breaks out, it cuts across and cuts up the already existing communities. The stronger the community of workers in struggle, the more the religious, national, ethnic, neighborhood, and craft communities look thin and archaic.

When we're stronger, more unified, more organized, more militant, we can more effectively fight for our interests and win real concessions. But it's not a simple matter of making demands, organizing, and then getting concessions. Class war is not like conventional war. Two sides do not meet on the battlefield and gain and lose ground. The interests, weapons, objectives, and edges of a community of workers in struggle are not simply set from the beginning.

A strike can be an expression of working-class power. It can also

WAGE CUTS   RENT INCREASES

ORGANIZING
STRIKES
DIRECT ACTION
EXPROPRIATION

skill, or experience, demands that link our pay to the profitability of the businesses we work for in various ways. More often, though, community leaders, union bureaucrats, or politicians will make these demands on our behalf. The more we take profitability and the "needs of the economy" as given, the more we are defeated before we begin.

Any government or political system is based on compromises between capitalists in different industries, different politicians, different community leaders, and different sections of the working class. These compromises are based on a set level of exploitation, a set distribution of value and surplus value. Economic crisis and the pressures of competition force the capitalist class to rearrange these compromises and attack our standard of living. Working-class struggles tend to disrupt these compromises by pushing in the opposite direction. Class war keeps coming back.

Faced with a serious working-class threat, the capitalists of any country will respond with some mix of reforms and repression, co-optation and marginalization. They don't much care what we've demanded or whether we've demanded anything.

NEW TECHNOLOGIES
INSTITUTIONALIZATION
REFORMS
CONCESSIONS
CO-OPTATION

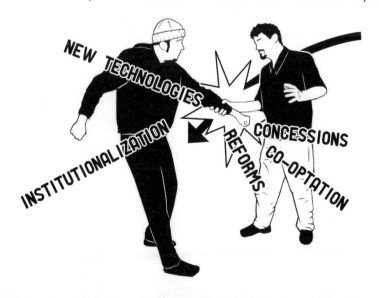

REPRESSION

attitudes that were previously seen as a threat to the system are neutralized and made into a part of the system. The terrain of class struggle shifts. Gains are turned into defeats. Some of the old communities and prejudices reassert themselves. Some new ones are formed. The community of struggling workers is fragmented. Progress within capitalism is built on the back of class struggles defeated in this way.

The next time we press our needs against the "needs of the economy" the shapes and strategies of a community of workers in struggle will have to adapt as well. We have to critique both the "failures" and the "successes" of previous movements or be quickly defeated.

Capitalism can bend, but it can't bend into any shape, and it can't bend as easily in any direction. The more we push and pull, the more clearly we see the shape of capitalist social relationships: what is essential, what isn't, how things relate to each other. Certain demands and reforms are not easily incorporated or begin to erode immediately. Capitalism pushed in certain directions quickly snaps back. Capitalism is based on class struggle but it is also based on one side always eventually winning.

Their goal is to end the disruption caused by our struggles. The question for them is what reforms will best keep us under control. They need to break up the community we've built up during and through the fight or harness it to the needs of capital accumulation. They will give concessions to one part of the movement and repress another part. They'll legalize one part and criminalize another. They'll promote some and fire others.

If we're strong enough and unified enough, we can force reforms that are actually at the expense of profitability. We can force changes that haven't been done before or that push and pull the system in new and different directions. These kinds of reforms are bitterly fought by the capitalists.

Still capitalism is adaptable. Governments can be replaced. Laws can be changed. Major reforms are possible. Reforms that push capitalism to adapt and progress can become a relatively permanent part of the system. The balance of forces are rearranged, the community of workers in struggle is cut across, and exploitation takes on a different shape. Organizations, groups,

NEW SOCIAL PEACE

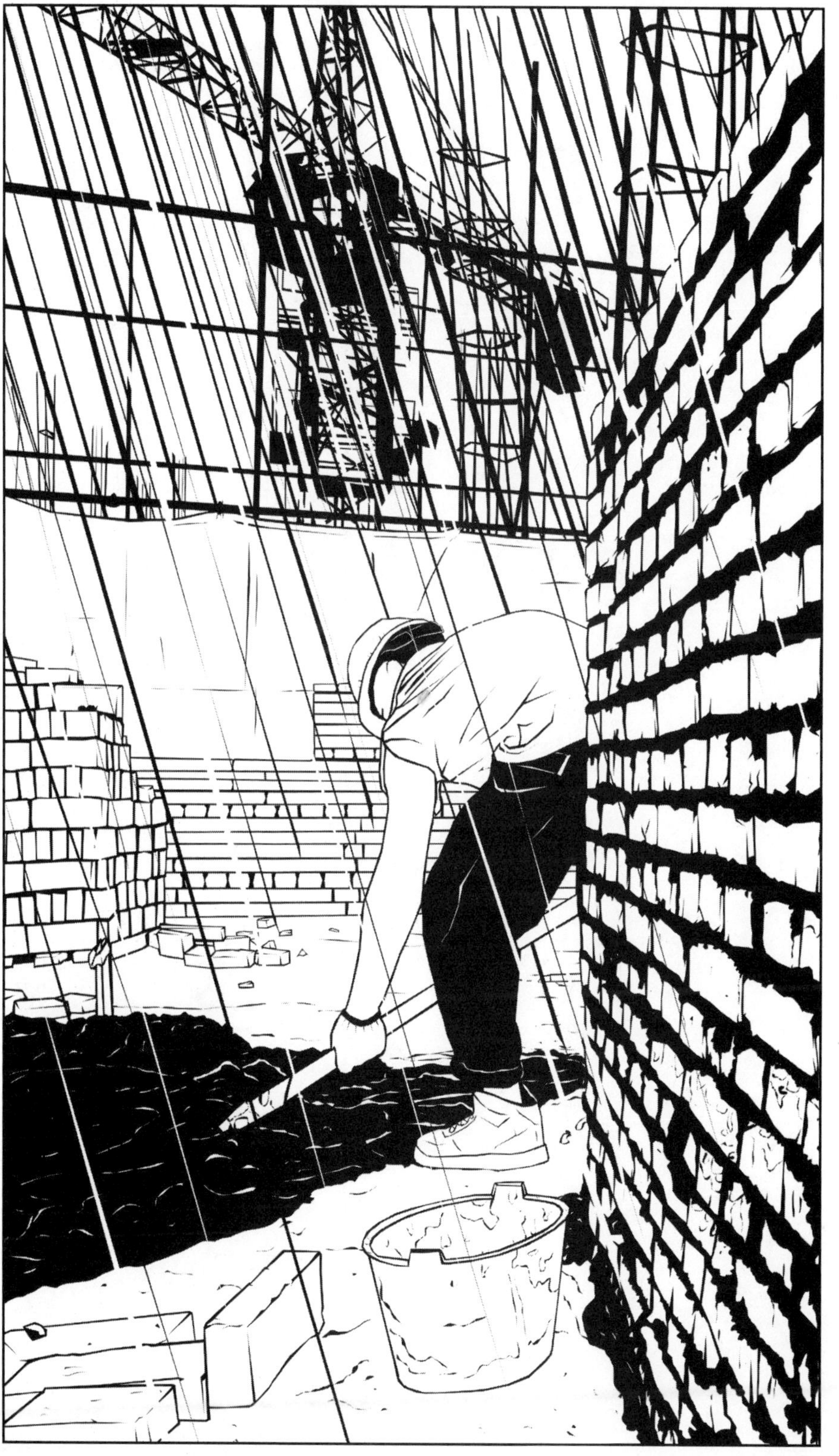

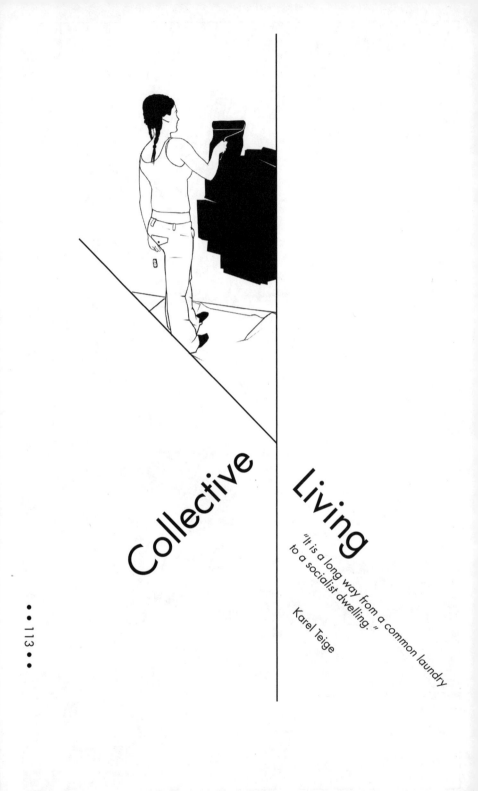

Collective

Living

"It is a long way from a common laundry to a socialist dwelling."

Karel Teige

Looking at the overwhelming isolation of modern suburban housing, of hundreds of individuals and families cooking food, doing laundry, watching TV, staring at computers for hours by themselves, it's easy to feel nostalgia for a more communal way of living. But modern privacy and separation hasn't replaced family living—it works on top of it. The same cities where individuals live alone in the suburbs also have people who live with their parents until they have children of their own—or longer—and 3 or 4 generations are living together in the same household. This is real community—real community that tends to impose social conformity, to be conservative and to overlap with strict and restrictive religion. Market isolation and fragmentation and conservative community play off each other. The teenager wants to get out of her parents' house as fast as possible. The middle-aged man gets married just so he's not alone. To be a full grown-up means to be alone—or alone with a family. Collective living outside the family is usually looked on as something for students, or maybe for young people just getting started with their lives, but not a particularly good idea.

In the family household, cooking, cleaning, entertainment, and other daily activities are direct and within the small community of the family. For the individual living alone, these activities tend to take place as part of a larger group—the city block, the neighborhood, the city—but are no longer direct. The community is lost and they tend to be simple market transactions—the laundromat, the restaurant, the bar, the movies.

Since early capitalism, workers have packed themselves into small living places and split the rent. They may have still hoped to one day have a nice little individual cottage with a wife and kids and a garden, but their practical responses to their situation pointed in a different direction. Market forces continued to erode family life and the reaction against this—the "traditional" family—showed itself to be restrictive and conservative. The obvious response was to look for some other kind of organized collective living.

Unions, socialist parties, progressive architects, public health officials, early feminists and artists came up with all sorts of ideas for collective living situations for the working class. In the more ambitious ones, private and family living space was restricted, and whole apartment blocks had integrated collective kitchens, gardens, laundries, sports facilities and self-defense classes, libraries, day care, and schools.

These achieved some important social changes. As housework was collectivized and centralized, it meant that there was less of it to do and it could be done all at once by fewer people. This and collective child care and schools freed women up to participate in work, sports, and political activities. Where possible, dense architecture reinforced the communal atmosphere, and shared

•• 114 ••

meals and other activities created lively communities around these collective apartment buildings.

These communities were of course denounced from all sides. Having unmarried women living in a building with men they weren't related to was "promiscuous." Having collective day care was "unnatural." Collective schools (often run by socialists) were "ungodly." Collective eating, laundry, and even front doors were "an attack on the individual" and dangerously "socialist." Against these attacks, collective living could be seen as a model that anticipated some future society where people lived and worked in collectives, and market forces had been tamed and socialized.

But just as the democratic, self-management of a business doesn't free it from the need to compete and exploit its employees, collective living does not free the inhabitants from the need to buy or rent land and buildings. By building densely and having collective facilities, some money was saved. But this did very little to eliminate the gap between what the average worker could afford and the price of decent housing.

Without subsidies, collective housing is only slightly more affordable than free market housing and tends only to be filled with the best-paid workers. Where tenants split the cost of the housing according to need, there is an incentive to only look for new tenants who can afford high rent, to subsidize the other tenants' rent. Alternately, housing costs can be brought down by having tenants do unpaid construction work—a strategy that can easily bring collective housing into conflict with construction workers and construction unions. Where collective living situations have really taken off and housed anything more than a tiny part of the working class, it is not through self-help and mutual aid, but with large subsidies and support from governments that had been taken over by socialist parties with an ideological commitment to collective living.

Today socialist parties don't even pretend to oppose capitalism anymore, and state intervention in the economy is accepted across the political spectrum. State spending on housing is much more likely to support family homeownership than any type of collectives or co-ops. The only remnant of an ideological commitment to collective living is with the semi-anarchist youth in whose collective houses the price of cheap rent is having to sit through excruciating consensus meetings or eat near-rotten food.

Anyone today who said that apartment buildings lead to a socialist mentality would be laughed at. The massive concrete housing towers in Novi Beograd are bought and sold just like the somewhat less massive concrete housing towers on Chicago's South Side. Even the rich are sometimes attracted to collective living. Sprawling suburban gated communities are located around an artificial pond and have quaint footpaths connecting them. Downtown condos use the community that allegedly forms around the pool in the basement, the common weight room, or yoga classes as a selling point.

Be the change!

Isolation and conservative, traditional community are still the normal state of things, but collective living is no longer seen as a threat. Detached from a militant workers' movement, collective housing easily becomes a marginalized commodity. Simply living differently is a failed strategy.

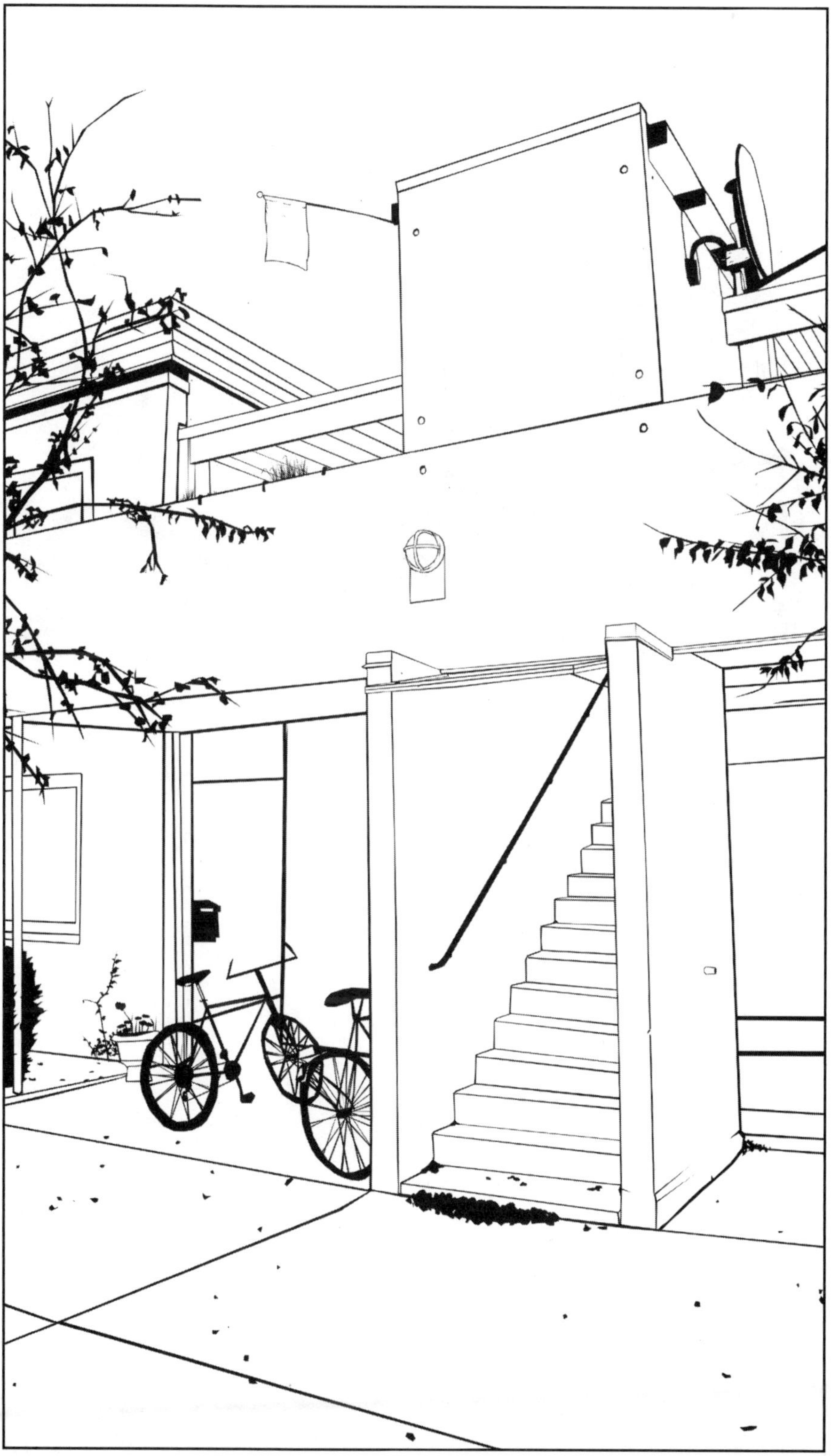

The Unions

"A CIO contract is adequate protection against sit-downs, lie-downs, or any other kind of strike."

John L. Lewis

Occasionally unions have made demands of governments or employers for better housing conditions. On the other hand, housing reforms have also often been seen as throw-away concessions, meant to distract from the main issues of wages, hours, and conditions. Although there have been unions that have built housing for their members, they usually have found this to be a dangerous investment. If they go on strike, not only do they not get regular dues from the striking workers, but they also stop getting regular rents. For these reasons (except where unions have been completely integrated into the state) the unions have mainly affected the relations between people making the houses—the production side, not the consumption side of the housing monster.

The nature of the building industry gives construction workers some basic advantages. Because house building still depends on the knowledge and decisions of skilled workers, we are more difficult to replace, and in a better bargaining position. Also, housing still can't usually be built in one place and shipped to where it's needed. This means that construction companies can't pick up their operations and move to the spot on the globe with the cheapest construction worker wages. It also means that the housing market is largely local or regional, so construction companies can give in to wage increases without having to worry about competing with low cost producers a thousand miles away. (However, if there's a depressed rural area or another country nearby with cheaper workers, they can sometimes be shipped in daily or weekly.)

But the shape of the building industry also creates problems for us. Workers are divided along craft lines and working for different bosses or subcontractors. Also, both within and between trades, there are important divisions (in pay and working conditions) between skilled and unskilled workers. This makes it less likely that different workers will have the same experiences, problems, and demands and will identify with each other, which makes it more difficult to organize and take action together.

Construction workers were among the first workers to form organizations to fight for their interests. These "unions"—"brotherhoods," "associations," "friendly societies," "conspiracies"—were diverse. They called strikes, sabotaged building

sites, beat up scabs, negotiated with the employers, brought in socialist speakers, held dances, ran libraries, gave their members healthcare and unemployment insurance, paid for funerals of workers killed on the job or on picket lines, and generally tried to represent the working man.

Over time a mixture of militant strikes, economic and political crisis, and the fear of revolution forced employers to bargain with the unions and make a range of reforms. Union representatives were legally recognized. Bargaining procedures were written into law. Workers organizing at work were given a legal definition and some legal protections. What it meant to be a union narrowed.

One of the most important reforms won by construction workers was the union hiring hall. Instead of working directly for a contractor, many construction workers get work through their union. Contractors tell the unions how many of which kinds of workers they need, and the unions send out workers—usually in order of seniority, who has been unemployed the longest and who showed up to the hall that morning. This is a major rearranging of the balance of power between employer and employee.

The boss can't move us around from job to job to keep us from talking to each other. A worker who gets in a fight with the company's foreman can quit on the spot and be reassigned to a new job the next day. The amount of crap we have to take from asshole bosses is greatly reduced. Hiring halls can also allow us more flexibility, and make it easier to take time off.

The hiring hall is an important limit on the boss's authority over his workers, but has advantages as a management strategy as well. Skilled workers are often difficult to find and replace. By going to a hiring hall, the boss can find whatever workers he needs without wasting time and money posting job ads and doing interviews. Apprenticeship and training programs are often jointly run by the unions and the building contractor associations. This means that the pool of workers available through the union have standardized skills, and contractors don't have to spend much time training new employees.

Reforms such as hiring halls are fought or accepted by employers—or fought, then accepted. There is a mixture of reforms and erosion of the reforms that can't be made functional for capital. Often

this simply creates labor market segmentation. The most skilled, best paid, most difficult to replace workers are organized in unions and work on commercial, government, and large-scale residential jobs. Less skilled, cheaper workers, doing smaller,

with employers and by controlling apprenticeship programs. They try to make themselves necessary middlemen, so workers need to go to them to get a job and employers need to go to them to get workers. When the union leadership and the workers

non-government jobs are not in unions. And at the edge of the labor market, repairs, small remodels, and additions are done by self-employed construction workers, or workers doing side work.

Union hiring halls tend to make the class relationship less personal. They don't change it. More work rules tend to be negotiated between union bureaucrats and contractors' associations, as opposed to between the boss and the worker on the spot (although how rules are actually followed and enforced is another thing). In either case, we still have to get up every day and work for them.

The construction unions that run hiring halls tend to become essentially labor brokerages. They try to control as much of the workforce as possible through exclusive deals

come into conflict, this control over access to work can be used against us, and militant or disruptive workers can be denied work.

Whatever the claims of socialists in the labor movement, unions are not defensive organizations of the working class. Their focus is much narrower. The unions are concerned with their membership, who are workers at a specific company (or a specific trade in a specific region). This limit may begin as a simple strategic starting point, but it means that workers from different unions, or workers in unions and those not in unions can get pitted against each other. The construction unions are some of the worst here, because they organize on a narrow craft basis. The workers on a particular construction site can easily belong to a dozen different unions. This limits the pressure workers can put on contractors, let alone a developer. As the unions are legally recognized, this craft separation is reinforced, often with laws against solidarity between workers in different unions. This can easily mean that the unions are required to make sure their workers cross other unions' picket lines.

"Yes, we can."

The unions might not actively fight each other for turf, or actively harm the interests of workers who aren't members. They may not go as far as the United Farm Workers of America under Cesar Chavez (who organized patrols of the US-Mexico border to keep out undocumented workers who might compete with their members for jobs or be used as scabs). But they definitely do not defend the interests of the working class in general.

And the unions don't just defend the interests of their members either. The workers in a union are not the union any more than the citizens of a country are the government. The unions have their own interests,

which may or may not coincide with the interests of the workers they represent at any time.

Union leaders perform a difficult balancing act. Their jobs are based on mobilizing us. They need to be seen as the head of a movement, the legitimate representatives. To do this they need to offer something to the membership—better wages, better conditions, more stable employment. They may even initiate certain types of struggles or support militant or illegal actions by workers in order to maintain their position. On the other side, they need to be recognized by the employers in order to get a contract. What they have to offer the employers is a workforce that's ready to work. The basis of the union contract is this compromise: employers give in to union recognition (and maybe other reforms) and the union agrees to keep its membership under control— to prevent strikes and disruptions of profit-making for the duration of the contract.

There is an arc to unionization. During the early stage of building a union, especially where the company and the government are opposed to unionization, the interests of the union leaders and the interests of the members can seem to be identical. The unions may be militant and intransigent. A real community of workers may be built by fighting the boss for a union. This community is built through the struggle. The unions are a partial expression of this struggle in an organization. But our power in the workplace doesn't come from being organized, but from being disruptive. As unions win contracts and are accepted as negotiators, the struggle has to end. If they want contracts, the unions have to clamp down on disruptiveness. The unions have to make proposals for how businesses should be run and to develop a spirit of compromise. Even when they don't completely sell us out, their negotiations are about how capital accumulation should be managed. This necessarily increases the distance between them and us. Where unions are thoroughly incorporated into the management of capitalist society (in a country, a city, or a particular business), they end up spending a lot of time enforcing the contract on their own workers. This means heading off, marginalizing, short-circuiting, and undermining any kind of militancy from the rank and file.

It's not that the unions sell us out and try to break up militancy because they're undemocratic, or controlled by politicians or mobbed-up bureaucrats. The separation between union bosses and union members tends to develop for the same reason that a separation between workers and bosses tends to develop. Businesses need to be competitive. They need to keep costs low. They need to make us work harder for less. The interests of capital and labor are fundamentally contradictory. Any kind of workers organization is eventually presented with a choice: fight for our interests or be a responsible part of managing capital. Even the most democratic organization that takes workers at

work as its starting and ending point, will ultimately be forced to support things that are against our interests.

With or without unions, the basic class relationship means that construction workers have to keep selling ourselves on the labor market. On a daily basis, we tend to be detached and pragmatic about whether or not to join unions. We know that you often get better pay and more benefits in the union, and that working through a union usually means that the pace or work won't be ridiculously fast and there is less likely to be piecework. At the same time, unions often have long apprenticeship programs, and may make it more difficult to move to a new area and have our skills and cards recognized. There also may not be as much work through the union hiring halls as through private employers, and the unions will require us to work exclusively through them.

When there are not major struggles going on, we tend to see the unions roughly the same way we see working for a boss who's a nice guy. When there are, we need to quickly go beyond the control of the union, or the movement is dampened, dissipated, and defeated.

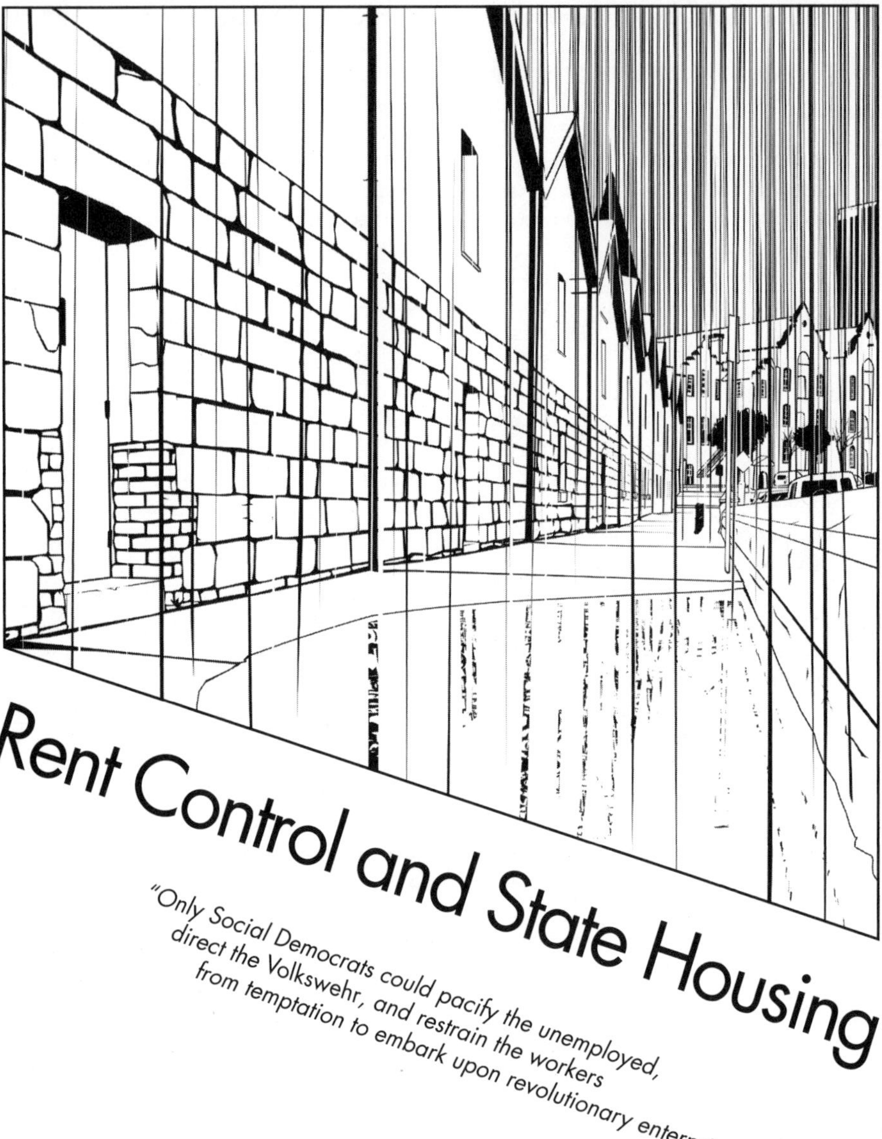

Rent Control and State Housing

"Only Social Democrats could pacify the unemployed, direct the Volkswehr, and restrain the workers from temptation to embark upon revolutionary enterprises..."

Otto Bauer

The free market in housing is supported and regulated by the state. Various levels of government impose all sorts of health and safety regulations, building codes, subsidies, taxes, tax subsidies, loan guarantees, and zoning laws that affect housing. The state does not intervene on behalf of the poor or interfere in the business of the rich. It tries to stabilize and unify a society that tends toward separation, fragmentation, and crisis. It balances the demands of developers, financiers, contractors, landlords, and "the public"—of capital invested in the land and the rest of capitalist society.

Normally the only interest the state has in controlling rents is in keeping high rents from putting too much pressure on employers to raise wages. Politicians will often use rent control that only applies to a tiny part of the housing stock, or that only puts very weak limits on rent increases to show they're doing something for the workin' man. Without a threat from below, the situation tends to be either low wages and low rents, or decent wages and high rents.

When such a threat exists, it's a different story. The agitation, strikes, mutinies, insurrections, and revolutions that happened during and immediately after the First World War were responded to with all kinds of reforms. This was the beginning of serious rent control.

In New York City, for example, landlords had taken advantage of wartime shortages to jack up the rents on apartments all over the city. In 1918 and 1919, thousands of tenants went on rent strike, supported rent strikes, and joined the growing tenants leagues in the city. The actions succeeded in stopping some rent increases and evictions. By 1920, there were fears that so many renters would refuse to pay rent that the police and the national guard simply couldn't evict them all, and New York passed tenant protections including limits on rent increases.

In 1915, in Glasgow, working-class tenants responded to rent increases by only paying the old

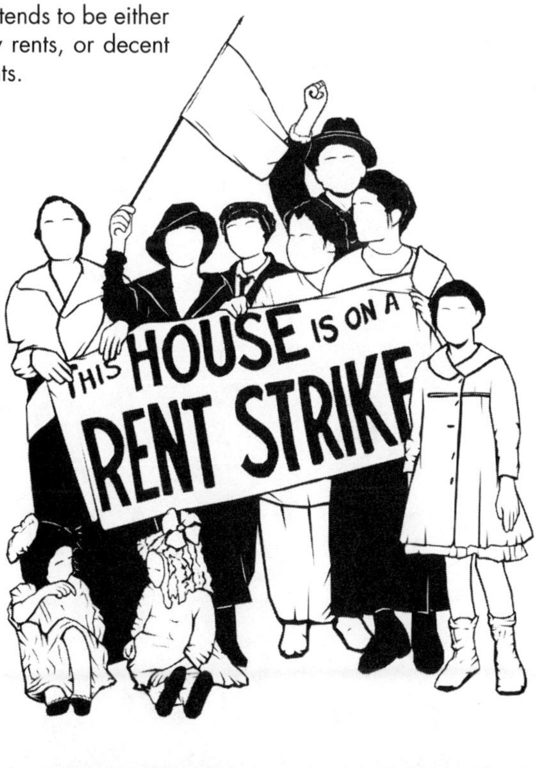
THIS HOUSE IS ON A
RENT STRIKE

rent or not paying any rent at all. Massive demonstrations kept the police from evicting people for not paying rent. The UK government, afraid that the rent strikes would lead to strikes in the Glasgow munitions factories, instituted national rent control.

Tenant protections are passed to protect against tenants' movements. Rent control is passed to control working-class renters.

But capital's movements are not a simple matter of government legislation. Limits on a landlord's right to evict tenants or on abuses like key money and security deposits are real gains, but they do not necessarily hurt capital invested in renting out houses. Especially when the market is stable, the landlord doesn't need to constantly evict tenants, and there are usually ways to get around the laws (like moving a family member into the apartment for a few months). Effective rent control is different. By definition, effective rent control has to limit landlords' profits. Since being a landlord, like any other line of business, is about making a profit, effective rent control makes renting houses a less competitive business. At first this may just mean that landlords try to make up the difference by spending less on repairs and maintenance. The longer the rent control lasts, the more incentive there is for landlords to put their money into some other business. Serious rent control that lasts for any amount of time necessarily leads to disinvestment in housing.

Rent control is a legal maximum price on a commodity. It pushes the flows of value, as different lines of business compete for investment. Usually an industry whose product is in high demand can raise its prices and attract more capital. Where there is serious rent control, real demand for houses will move above supply, but prices can't rise. Either the rent control will be repealed, or a black market will tend to develop, where housing is rented out at above legal levels—which undermines the effectiveness of the rent control. If the black market is cracked down on, and house rents are strictly kept at the rent controlled level, it won't just be the landlord business that will become uncompetitive. As capital moves out of the business of renting housing, the market for houses shrinks. Developers and construction companies see their profits squeezed, which leads to disinvestment in house production generally. In time, this causes housing shortages. The state is then

rent control
black market

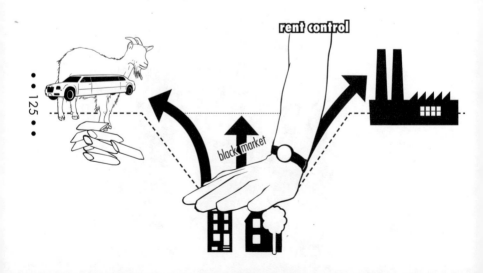

faced with a choice: peel back the rent control, face a housing crisis, or go into the landlord business itself.

A certain kind of state housing is a normal compliment to the free market in housing. This is housing that is recognized as only for the very poor. Often it is falling apart, and usually has restrictive or humiliating rules. Rent collection may be combined with apartment inspections. There may be curfews or restrictions on visitors. It may be limited only to proper families— married couples with children. Tenants' privacy is rarely respected. This kind of state housing works as a constant reminder to the rest of the working class that we could be worse off. It stops working this way, the moment it becomes a desirable place to live for anyone other than the extremely poor—the moment it starts to compete with private landlords.

Usually the place where the state is most willing to compete with private landlords is where it is also the employer. In this case, it has a direct interest in keeping rents from putting upward pressure on wages. The first kind of housing that states built was often for their soldiers and for workers in key nationalized industries. Where it goes further than that, where the government starts building for the working class in general, where government housing actually competes with private landlords, it only does so in response to a serious crisis and strong working-class movements that need to be co-opted.

The state will act as landlord, but it still buys the land from private owners (pays capitalized rents), hires private contractors to do the building, and borrows the money from banks or in the form of bonds (and so has to pay interest). Where the government owns enough land, or has strict enough land use laws, land speculation can be severely

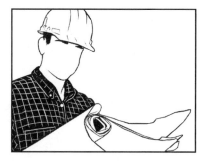

limited. Assuming that state housing does not operate for a profit, the price of housing can be lowered. In this case, the landlord has been sacrificed for the good of capitalist society in general.

On top of this, the state may provide subsidies, further lowering the price of housing. These subsidies, if permanent and regular, are essentially a collectivized form of wage increase. Instead of money paid directly to employees for working, the money is paid to the state (through higher taxes), who then distributes it in socialized benefits. This is a real, material gain, just like subsidies to lower public transit costs, or free government healthcare. Just like a wage increase, it can improve the quality of housing we can afford. Since socialized housing is given to people equally (skilled workers don't usually get better state housing than unskilled), it tends to lessen the differences between rich and poor neighborhoods and to slow the creation of slums and ghettos.

Still, having the state pay part of our rent is expensive. The authorities may give in to this when they feel threatened. As a movement is repressed and institutionalized, the threat fades. Subsidies tend to be taken away. Private landlords may reappear. State housing may deteriorate and start to be seen as only for the very poor once again.

On the other hand, state housing can become a regular part of the functioning of capitalist society. Tenants' unions can get state funding and become a respectable part of managing the housing stock, negotiating rents with the government. Where the state acts as a nonprofit landlord, part of the gain in lowered rents can go to employers in the form of lower wages. In certain times and places businesses have supported state housing, as a way to keep wages low—especially businesses that produce for export. In the same way, a business may support government healthcare so that it can be in a better position when competing with businesses in countries where healthcare benefits are paid for by employers. One part of capital profits off another part's problems.

Also, just because the state is not making a profit, does not mean that landed capital has been eliminated. As development happens and housing prices go up, the benefit to working-class tenants shrinks. Where the state pays private companies their costs plus a "fair profit," there's an incentive for them to just jack up their prices and make more profit. While the state may simply be increasing rents to cover its costs, the increased rents are going to construction contractors or the manufacturers of building materials, or the banks and investors (in the form of increased interest on loans).

State housing also has problems that private housing does not. Getting into state housing may mean proving our incomes are below a certain level, and usually means waiting on a list until a place opens up. Once we get a place, we're probably not going to be evicted unless we stop paying the rent, but if we leave, we'll probably have to wait a long time before finding a new place. People tend to stay in social housing as long as they can. Even if we're allowed to swap houses with other tenants in social housing or to get some sort of government certificate of urgency that allows tenants in a bad situation to jump the line for new apartments, it doesn't change the fact that government housing tends to reduce tenant mobility. And reduced mobility goes hand in hand with reduced wages, as we're not able to move to new places for new job opportunities. Where state housing goes along with wage compression (shrinking the difference between the lower and higher paid workers) this reduced mobility can help keep skilled workers from moving somewhere else for higher wages—and therefore help lower employers' labor costs.

The state is less likely to be a personally vindictive landlord or to demand huge rent increases, but it does not give us housing for free. Whether we pay rent to the local government or a private landlord, housing is still a commodity. The house is bought with money, and the need to come up with rent money is a major factor pushing us to go to work every day.

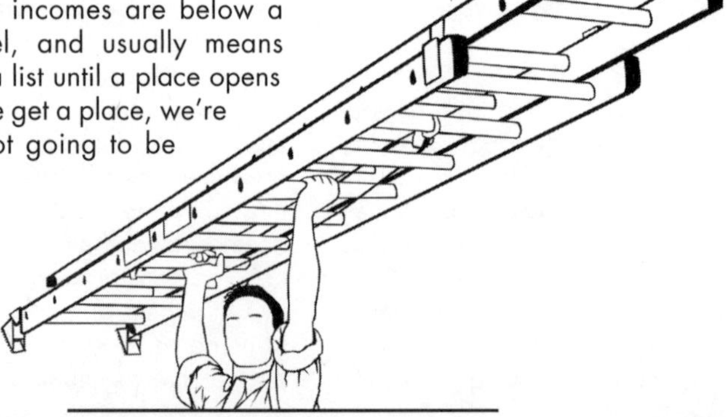

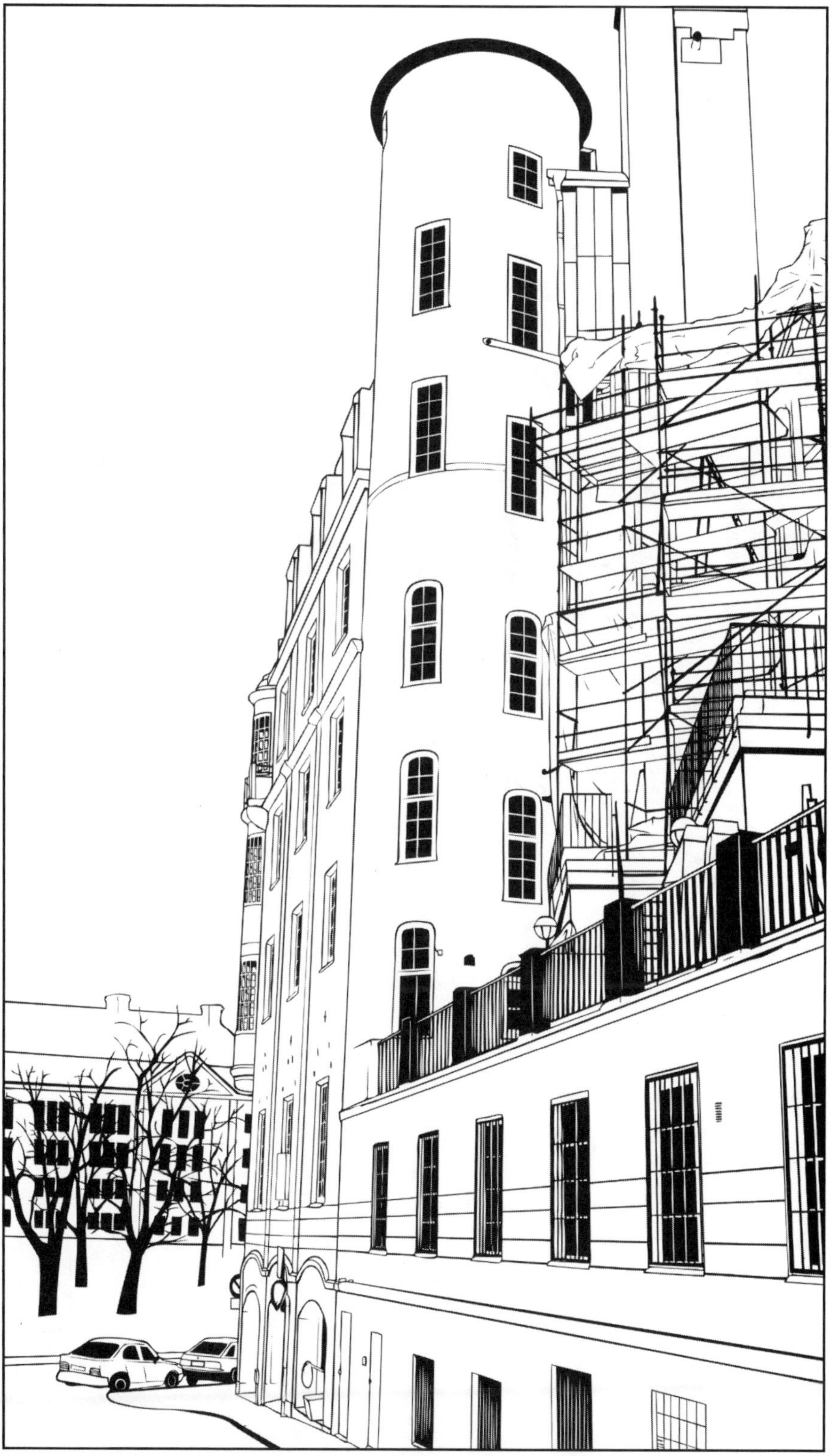

The Second World

"Russian capitalism, in
consequence of its lateness, its
lack of independence, and its resulting
parasitic features, has had much less time
than European capitalism technically to educate
the laboring masses, to train and discipline them for
production. That problem is now in its entirety imposed
upon the industrial organizations of the proletariat."

Leon Trotsky

In February of 1917, the Russian workers overthrew the Czar. There were massive strikes in Petrograd. There were several days of rioting. Police headquarters were looted and the workers armed themselves. When the army was called in to shoot down the striking workers, there were mutinies. Workers began to set up factory committees. Soldiers began to desert in huge numbers. The Czarist government collapsed and a parliamentary government came to power. The eight-hour day was instituted. Unions were legalized. But the government was weak. There was an unstable situation where powerful, armed workers' groups coexisted and competed with the government—neither in complete control of the situation.

In October, the parliamentary government was overthrown and the Bolsheviks took power with widespread support from the workers. Russia pulled out of the war. Buildings, factories, machines, and land owned by private business were taken over by the workers. Many private capitalists fled the country leaving the workers to run things themselves. There was real hope for a new world without class and exploitation.

By the summer of 1921 that hope was long gone. The power of the workers had been destroyed, and the new state had consolidated its power. Discipline in the army had been restored. The factory committees had been replaced by state-controlled unions. Strikes were illegal and strikers were jailed, shot, or denied food rations. The Communist Party was managing a strange form of capitalism.

There was no stock market and the banks were nationalized. As land was taken over by the workers and then by the state, land speculation was all but eliminated and very few people had to rent houses from private

landlords. Production was taken over by large state-owned enterprises. Production targets were set by the central government's plans. Prices were not set through free market competition, but were imposed by the state. The government stayed in power by a mixture of concessions to the working class and extreme police repression.

With private investment and speculation clamped down on, the "normal" business cycle was disrupted, and the central plan guaranteed a continuous source of demand for housing. This allowed construction firms to make the large investments necessary to industrialize house production. Factory-made cement slabs were assembled into apartment buildings, sometimes several blocks long. This meant that housing that used to take more than a year to build could be built in a few months. It also meant that fewer skilled workers were necessary. These prefab concrete housing blocks may not have been

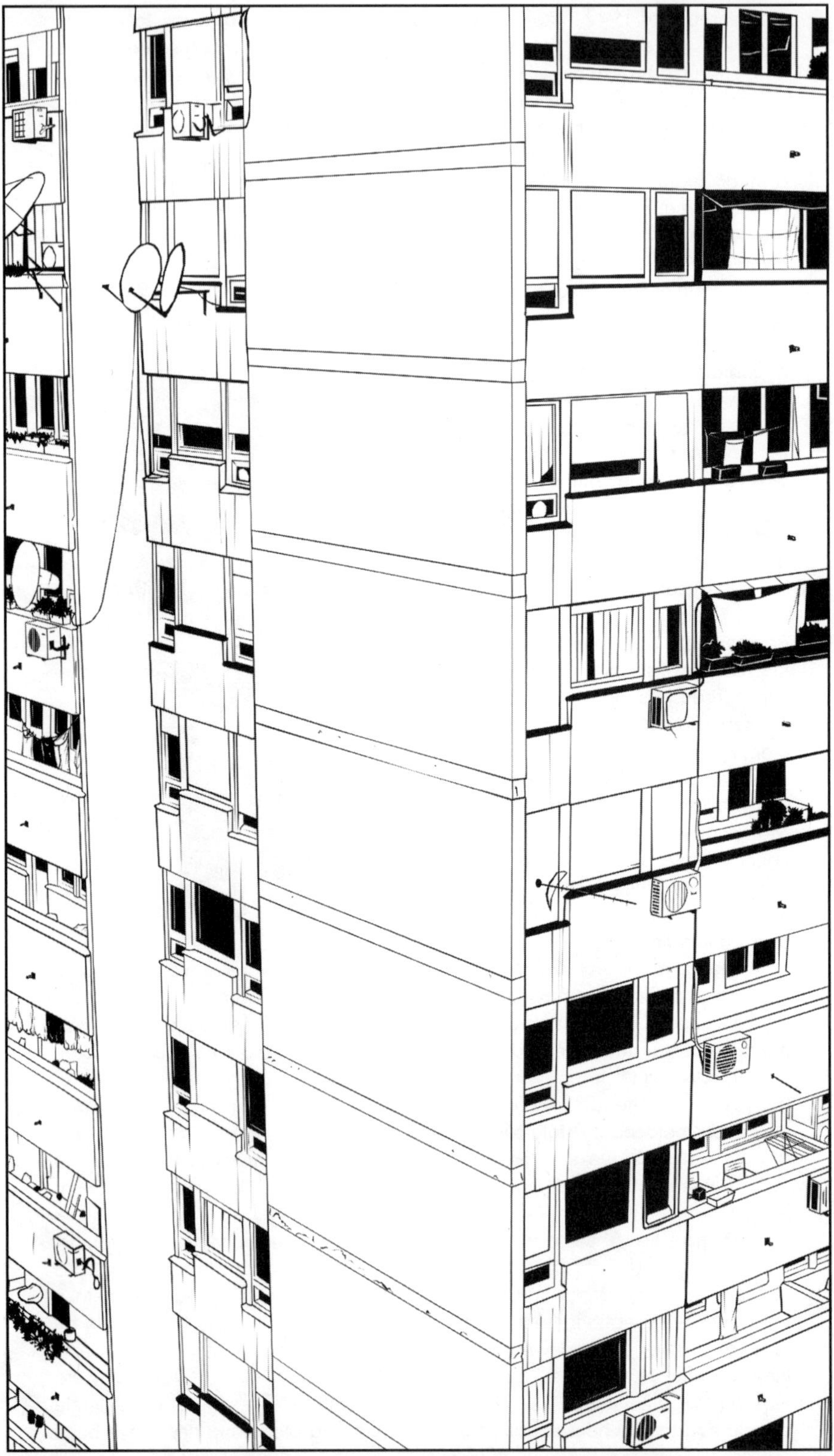

pretty, but they did bring down the cost of housing.

Even so, the rent that tenants were charged usually didn't even cover the maintenance costs of the buildings, let alone the construction costs. The state massively subsidized housing. This meant that the USSR often had the cheapest rents in the world, with workers often paying less than 5% of their income on rent.

The workers in the Soviet Union got a large part of their wages in a socialized form—free healthcare, free education, subsidized transport and housing. What was left of the individual hourly wage was a less strong incentive to keep them working hard. On top of that, the government was committed to a policy of full employment, there wasn't an unemployed population competing with those in work, and there were constant labor shortages. This meant that the fear of losing your job was a less effective way of getting the workers to work harder. The managers of state-owned enterprises needed to find alternative ways of putting pressure on the workers.

Housing was useful here. For those working for the key nationalized heavy industries, state housing was usually distributed through the employer. This worked like company housing. Skilled workers could be attracted and kept working for a firm by the promise of good housing. Strikers, workers slacking off on the job, and other troublemakers could be not

only fired, but evicted also. Workers who didn't get their housing from their employer most often got it through the municipal Soviet governments. But here too, workers who were thrown out of employer housing for breaking "labor discipline" were not allowed into other forms of state housing. And in both kinds of state housing, there were often long waiting lists to get an apartment. This created an incentive to stay in the same apartment and helped to reduce the turnover of skilled workers.

But not all housing was directly run by the state (local governments or nationalized firms). Plenty of people owned their own private houses, and the state-owned banks often provided low interest loans to people wanting to build houses for themselves. The state also provided loans for co-op construction, where people pooled their savings and had houses built and then owned their own place in the building. And the private landlord was never completely eliminated.

There were always landlords renting out rooms or whole houses, whether legally or on the black market.

Landlordism was regularly denounced in the papers. State housing was the norm. Co-ops were much more expensive and tended to be seen as a status symbol. Someone who paid the extra money for a co-op was housing themselves and freeing up state money for the building of socialism. They tended to be owned by skilled workers and party bureaucrats. Individual homeownership tended to be associated with backward rural people or unskilled workers living on the outskirts of the city who still wanted to have their own garden. The different types of housing were viewed very differently than in "the free world." Differences in tenure still overlapped and reinforced differences at work.

And at work, Russia was even more like America. Workers sold their ability to work to an employer. The firms sold the things that workers made and reinvested the money to enlarge production. Workers got enough to survive and keep working. The class relationship was the same, and work was just as alienating and miserable. Workers were no more motivated to work hard because management claimed to be socialist and the factories had red stars painted on them. Dead labor had to move and expand, and could only do so by exploiting workers. The management of factories in Russia used many of the same strategies as American businessmen to squeeze more surplus value out of the workers—piece work, time and motion studies.

The difference was that before the revolution, Russia was on the edge of the global economy, developing as an auxiliary to Western European and American capitalism. Although the communist elements of the revolution were quickly destroyed (largely by the Communist Party) the revolution had destroyed the power of private investors, bankers, and factory owners. The Russian state then wholeheartedly took the viewpoint of capital invested

in production. Everything was organized around the goal of quickly developing industry—especially heavy industry. The Soviet Union became a model for rapid industrialization. It was at times attractive to nationalists on the edges of world capitalism from Latin America to East Asia. The Second World seemed like a way of moving out of the Third World.

There was a strong commitment to collective forms of living left in

number of people and the time and distance people were commuting steadily increased. Extended families disintegrated and people increasingly lived in nuclear families. Housework was not eliminated and still fell mainly on women (party propaganda even glorified the role of the Soviet woman as mother and housewife at times). Home and work were increasingly separate in time and space. Being stuck at home was no less isolating than in "the free world." Having hiring centers on the ground floor of apartment blocks no more overcame

Russia after the Revolution. Housing blocks were built with shared repair shops, laundry and preschool facilities, dining rooms, and even kitchens. These, and new laws giving women legal equality, did mean women were much freer to participate in work and party political activities. Social life was being radically reorganized, but the changes were more the result of building modern capitalist society than of dismantling it.

Urbanization happened at a speed never before seen in world history. The

the contradictions between home and work than today's migrant Chinese construction workers have overcome these tensions by sleeping in tents on the construction sites where they work.

Value existed as a social relationship in Russia (and everywhere the Russian model was followed). Things did not get from the people who produced them to the people who needed them except by being bought and sold. Value still linked separate competing enterprises producing commodities. The workers in Soviet tractor factories and coal mines saw the things they were making as the property of someone else—the state firms—not just as useful things. Competition was severely limited, but not stopped.

Limiting competition allowed the central planners to protect and develop industry and to make some material concessions to the working class. Money capital did not siphon off all the surplus value from industry, and interest on state loans was low. The prices of many commodities (such as houses) were heavily subsidized. Prices were imposed, not formed by competition on the free market. A largely socialized wage and a sellers' labor market gave workers some power in the workplace. This meant that management often had trouble imposing new production methods and intensifying work. Caught between the hostility of the workers and the production quotas of the central planners, the quality of commodities suffered. Problems caused by defective products cascaded through the supply chain. There were shortages (especially of consumer goods). Prices could not rise to meet rising demand. There was rationing, long lines at the nearly empty shops and a widespread black market. Different firms tried to hoard resources, skilled workers, and centrally located plots of land, and bartered with each other and with local governments to get the resources they needed. The USSR was capitalist, but malfunctioning capitalism. And most of the rest of the Second World was less ambitious than the USSR had been.

The leading ideology of the First World claims that a businessman selling commodities is the same as the worker selling most of her waking hours. The dominant ideology of the Second World claimed to be classless as well. But the contradiction between the "needs of the economy" and the needs of the workers is where class comes from.

When the Cuban state paid employees of its nationalized industries their regular wages to build houses that would be rented to them at subsidized rates, it sold this as a plan to socialize property and benefit the workers. At the same time, the rest of the workers left at work had to sign agreements to maintain the same levels of production with fewer people working. Several years later, productivity had been raised in industry, and the government discontinued the construction "microbrigades" (regular construction worker wages were lower). Profits did not go into the hands of individual private capitalists, but the core problem of the economy was the same: how to squeeze as much surplus value out of the workers as possible.

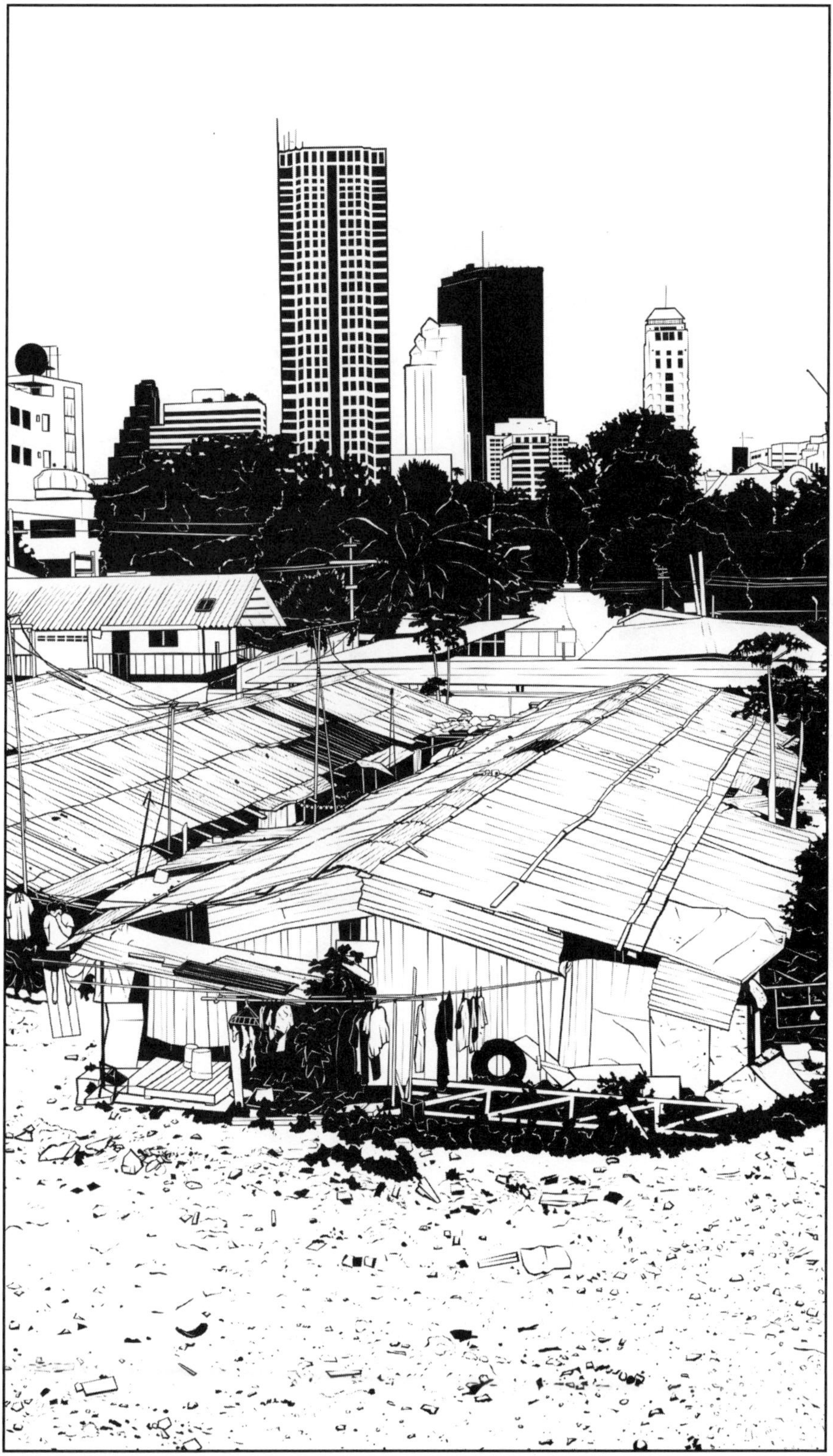

Getting Rid of Monsters

"Modern man wants meat without blood,
tobacco without nicotine,
commodities without sweat stains,
war without corpses,
police without truncheons,
truncheons without bruises,
money without speculation."

Gilles Dauvé

Whenever the need for a real critique of the system is strongly felt, distorted, self-defeating, pseudo-critiques multiply.

To complain about parasitic, speculative capital is to support good, productive, industrial capital. To complain about the "obscene profits" of big corporations is only to support the prudish profits of small businesses. To complain about the rich, white men who run the government, is to imply that the poor, woman of color, if put in the same situation, could do things differently. The billionaire whose company depends on there being masses of people so poor that they have nothing to sell but their ability to work—and who pays them just enough to keep them in that position—donates some of the profits he squeezes out of them to "alleviate poverty."

All the critiques of immoral businessmen or the attempts to set up ethical businesses do not make value flow through the economy according to ethical rules. Clichéd criticism of capitalism only works to make criticism of capitalism into a cliché.

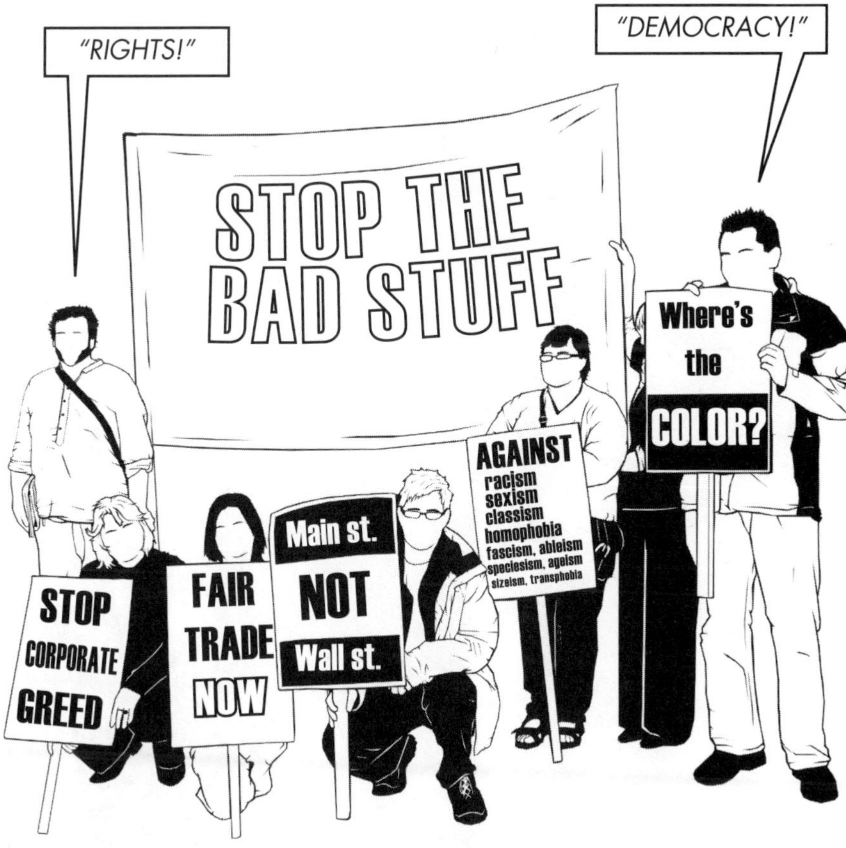
"RIGHTS!"
"DEMOCRACY!"
STOP THE BAD STUFF
Where's the COLOR?
AGAINST racism sexism classism homophobia fascism, ableism speciesism, ageism sizeism, transphobia
STOP CORPORATE GREED
FAIR TRADE NOW
Main st. NOT Wall st.

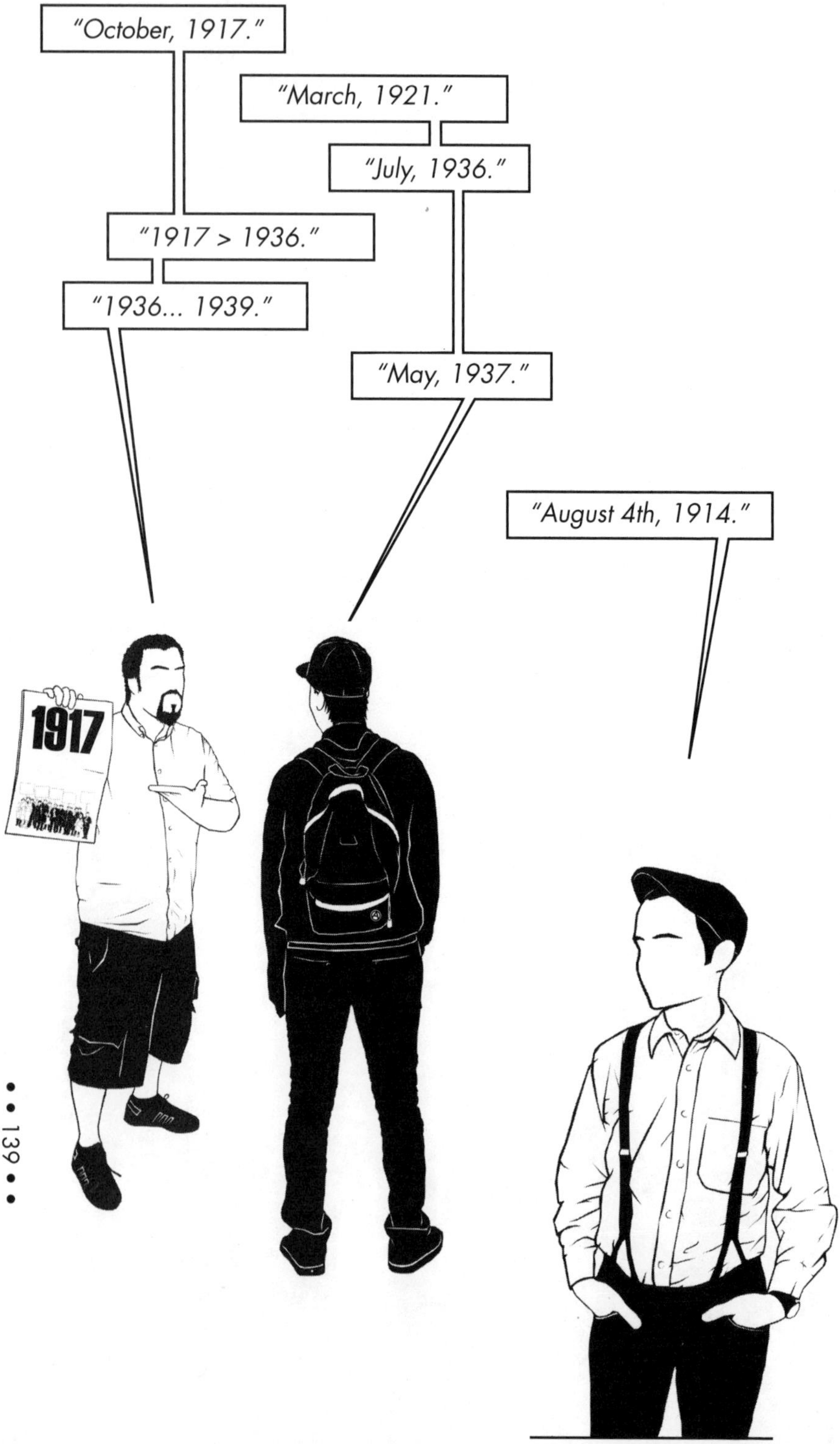
"October, 1917."
"March, 1921."
"July, 1936."
"1917 > 1936."
"1936... 1939."
"May, 1937."
"August 4th, 1914."
1917

Combine criticism with enough moralizing, and monsters appear everywhere—evil robber baron capitalists, lying politicians, greedy speculators, sadistic police, insane war criminals. Calling something a monster is admitting that you don't understand it. There are plenty of bosses, bankers, landlords, and developers that should probably be severely beaten in an alley somewhere, but demonizing them only covers up how the system continually recreates repressive police, asshole bosses, and two-faced politicians—not to mention weak, timid, prejudiced, and isolated workers.

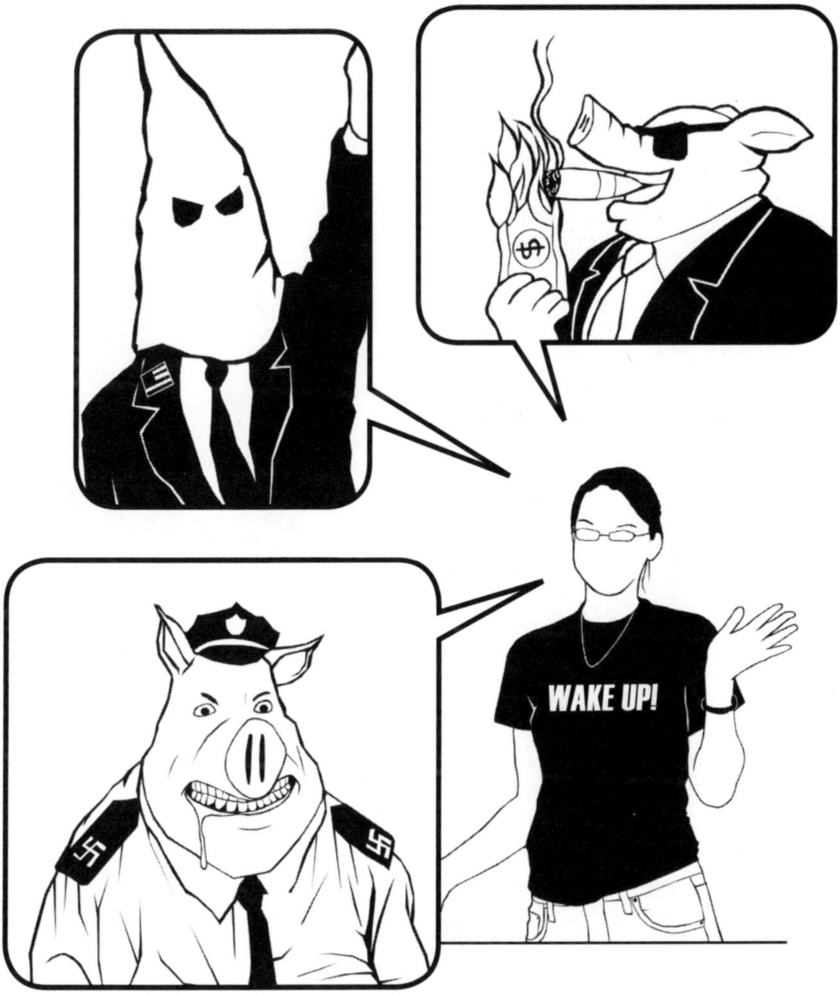
WAKE UP!

And half-critique can easily be turned into a dangerous caricature of itself. The response of the newspapers to the rent strikes, riots, and protests of working-class New York after WWI, was to denounce the evil "Bolsheviki Russian Jew landlord." More often, though, the leftists who explain the system only by its worst consequences just play into the hands of the politicians who denounce these consequences in the name of the system.

An important step in getting rid of monsters is to stop thinking of them as monsters.

"*Society is crushing the individual.*"

Capitalism means suburbs and slums, condos and ghettos. It means evictions and security deposits, cold, moldy, infested apartments, and high rent. It means repetitive, boring, dangerous work, unemployment, and homelessness. It means isolation, imaginary togetherness and real conservative communities, prejudice, racism, and political correctness. It means speculation and regulation, growth and stagnation, crisis and war. It means landlords and loan sharks, police and politicians, bureaucrats and bosses.

But all these things come about because they work. They grow out of and reinforce the basic capitalist social relationships. These social relationships are not optional. If we want food, housing, or anything else, we have to buy it, and the only way we have to make money is to sell our ability to work. The pressures we feel in everyday life are the same that explode in the wars and crisis that disrupt everyday life. Dead labor needs to squeeze living labor. Capital needs to move and expand. Our everyday activity is turned against us and seems like a force of nature, a monster.

ce sac est vert

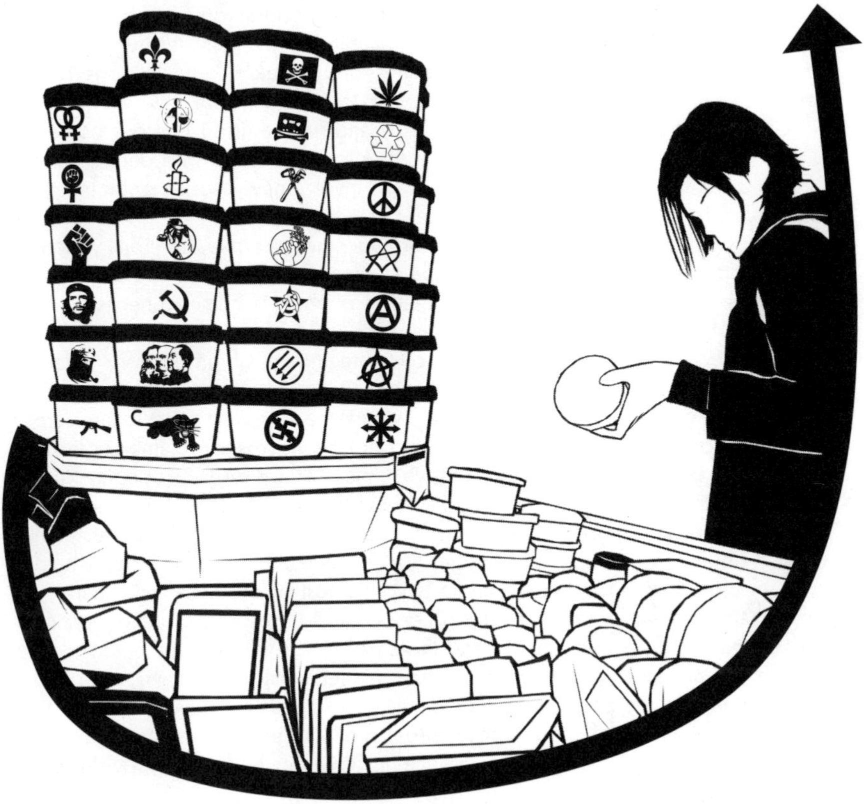

The more our lives are controlled by abstract forces beyond our control, the more a cult of personal responsibility grows. The more the "needs of the economy" impose choices on us, the more social behavior is treated as a moral issue. The more complex reality is, the more people want simple answers. We lash out at whoever is nearby. The system creates conflict that is at times slow and subconscious, at others spectacular and intense. This constant chaos and infighting keeps the system running.

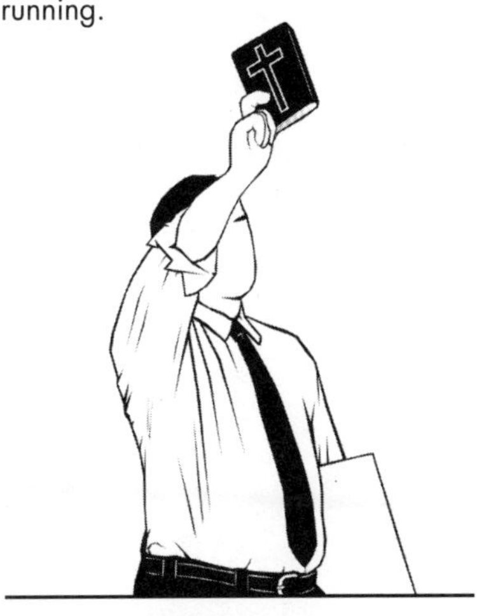

To the extent that we can see who our real enemies are, we can come together to fight for our interests. A community of workers in struggle can undermine ethnic or national communities and break down divisions and prejudices. Fighting side by side, we relate to each other in new ways, we discover abilities we didn't know we had, and we begin to feel our power. Demands are won (and often undermined). In order to grow and deepen, the struggle has to go beyond its previous limits, involve new people, and change strategies. It has to become more radical or stagnate.

As struggles develop and deepen, more becomes possible, horizons widen. At a certain point, when workers' struggles are pushing and pulling almost to the breaking point, a critique of the system as a whole becomes a necessity. In these revolutionary times, similar ideas about a future society have popped up.

In a society where no one could own the means of production, where things were available free for use, no one would be forced to sell their labor to someone else. This would be a society where there was no need to measure the value of things, because value would not be necessary to link separate commodity producers. People would have to make things directly for each other without their having to be bought and sold in between. This could only happen if productive activity was freely chosen and an expression of our lives, not forced on us in exchange for a wage. Making and doing useful things would not separate itself in time and space from the rest of our lives, and then try to take them over. In such a society, there could be no separate economy or government with its own needs, and there would be no need for bosses and police to enforce those needs. Constant conflict would not be necessary to divide and rule the population. Community would be possible everywhere in everyday life, not a defensive shell to retreat into. This perspective has appeared again and again where workers' movements have reached a certain point.

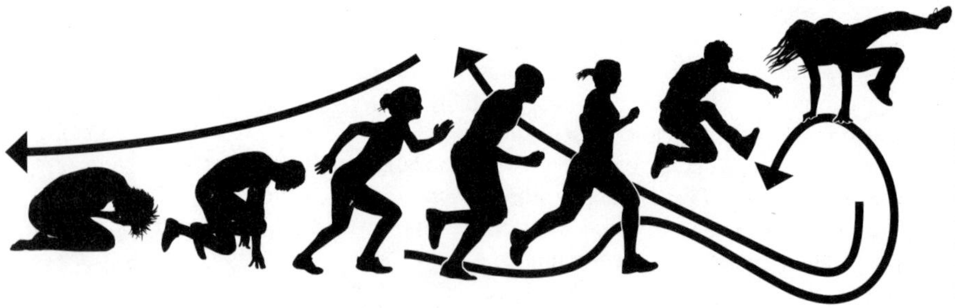

This is not about comparing the present to an imaginary classless, moneyless future and finding it lacking. It's about imagining what it would take to collectively stop living our lives the way we have been up till now. It's about developing our everyday struggles to the point where we're in a position to break capitalist social relationships once and for all. We need decisive ideas and elegant actions.

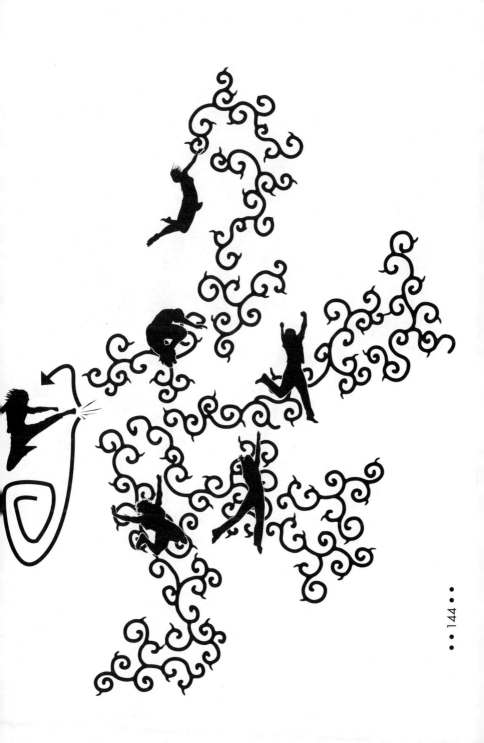

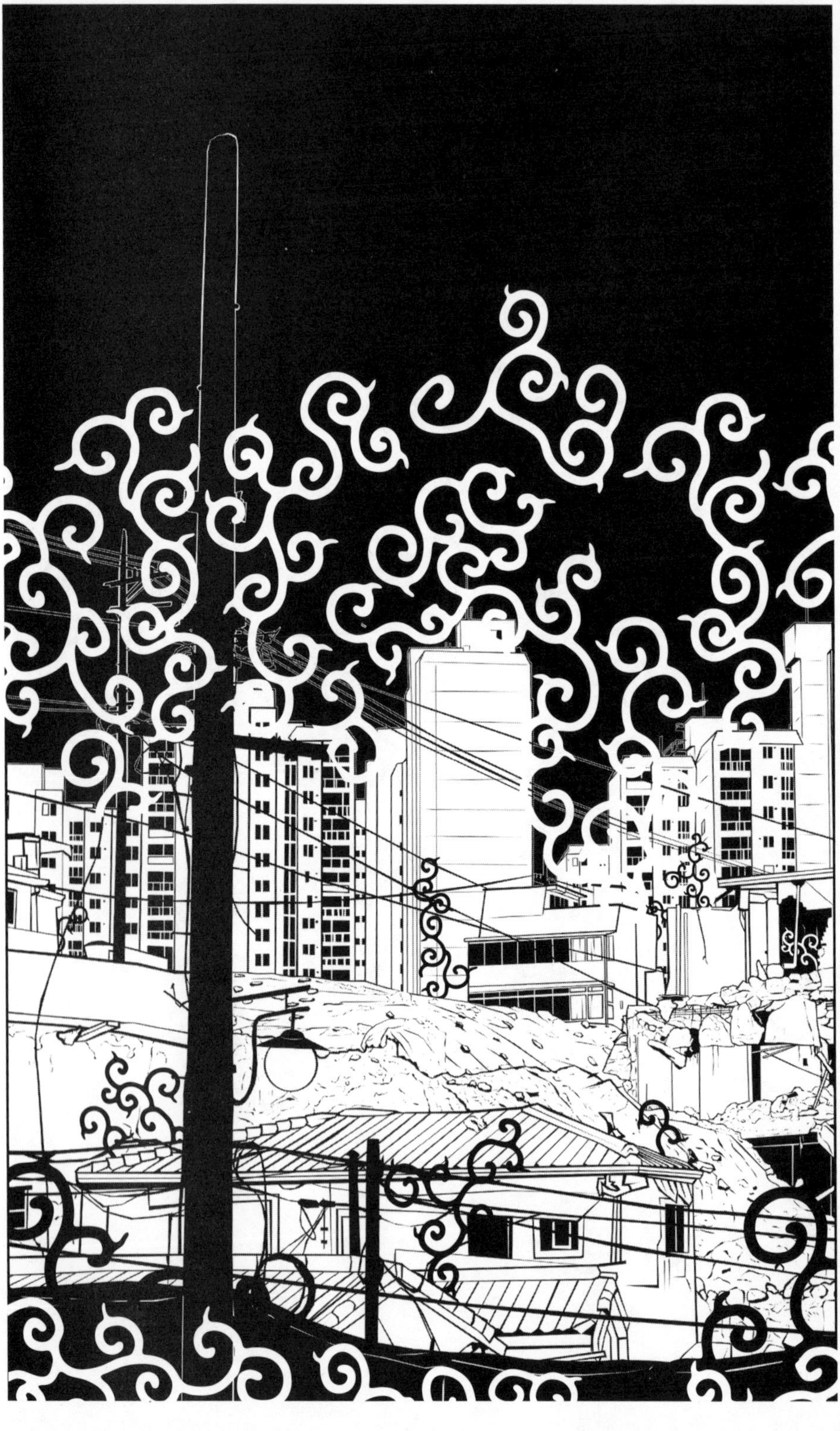

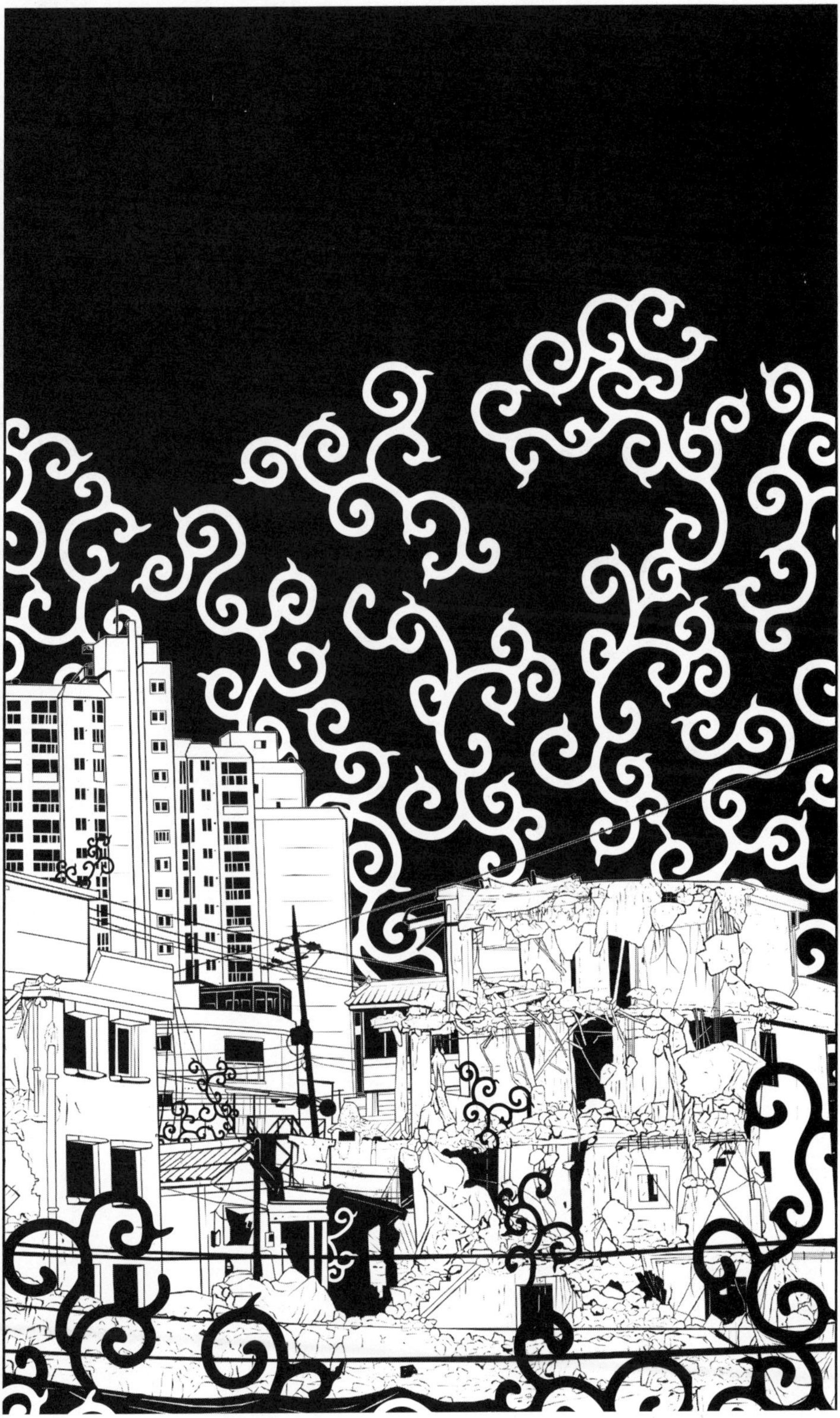

THANKS

to the following people for ideas, criticism, suggestions, proofreading, and modeling for *The Housing Monster*:

Claude-Catherine • Daniel from polkagris.nu • Ehssan • Gilles
Henrik from Malmö • Husunzi • Jack • Johan • Jonah
Joseph Kay • Kristen • libcom Steven • Patrick & Betsy
Pete from Australia • PM Press • Rik • Sabu
Sean from New Orleans • Vilemaxim

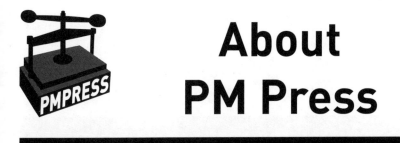

About
PM Press

politics • culture • art • fiction • music • film

PM Press was founded at the end of 2007 by a small collection of folks with decades of publishing, media, and organizing experience. PM Press co-conspirators have published and distributed hundreds of books, pamphlets, CDs, and DVDs. Members of PM have founded enduring book fairs, spearheaded victorious tenant organizing campaigns, and worked closely with bookstores, academic conferences, and even rock bands to deliver political and challenging ideas to all walks of life. We're old enough to know what we're doing and young enough to know what's at stake.

We seek to create radical and stimulating fiction and nonfiction books, pamphlets, t-shirts, visual and audio materials to entertain, educate, and inspire you. We aim to distribute these through every available channel with every available technology, whether that means you are seeing anarchist classics at our bookfair stalls; reading our latest vegan cookbook at the café; downloading geeky fiction e-books; or digging new music and timely videos from our website.

Contact us for direct ordering and questions about all PM Press releases, as well as manuscript submissions, review copy requests, foreign rights sales, author interviews, to book an author for an event, and to have PM Press attend your bookfair:

PM Press • PO Box 23912 • Oakland, CA 94623

510-658-3906 • info@pmpress.org

Buy books and stay on top of what we are doing at:

www.pmpress.org

FOPM

MONTHLY SUBSCRIPTION PROGRAM

These are indisputably momentous times—the financial system is melting down globally and the Empire is stumbling. Now more than ever there is a vital need for radical ideas.

In the four years since its founding—and on a mere shoestring—PM Press has risen to the formidable challenge of publishing and distributing knowledge and entertainment for the struggles ahead. With over 200 releases to date, we have published an impressive and stimulating array of literature, art, music, politics, and culture. Using every available medium, we've succeeded in connecting those hungry for ideas and information to those putting them into practice.

Friends of PM allows you to directly help impact, amplify, and revitalize the discourse and actions of radical writers, filmmakers, and artists. It provides us with a stable foundation from which we can build upon our early successes and provides a much-needed subsidy for the materials that can't necessarily pay their own way. You can help make that happen—and receive every new title automatically delivered to your door once a month—by joining as a Friend of PM Press. And, we'll throw in a free T-Shirt when you sign up.

Here are your options:
- $25 a month: Get all books and pamphlets plus 50% discount on all webstore purchases

- $40 a month: Get all PM Press releases (including CDs and DVDs) plus 50% discount on all webstore purchases

- $100 a month: Superstar—Everything plus PM merchandise, free downloads, and 50% discount on all webstore purchases

For those who can't afford $25 or more a month, we're introducing *Sustainer Rates* at $15, $10 and $5. Sustainers get a free PM Press t-shirt and a 50% discount on all purchases from our website.

Your Visa or Mastercard will be billed once a month, until you tell us to stop. Or until our efforts succeed in bringing the revolution around. Or the financial meltdown of Capital makes plastic redundant. Whichever comes first.

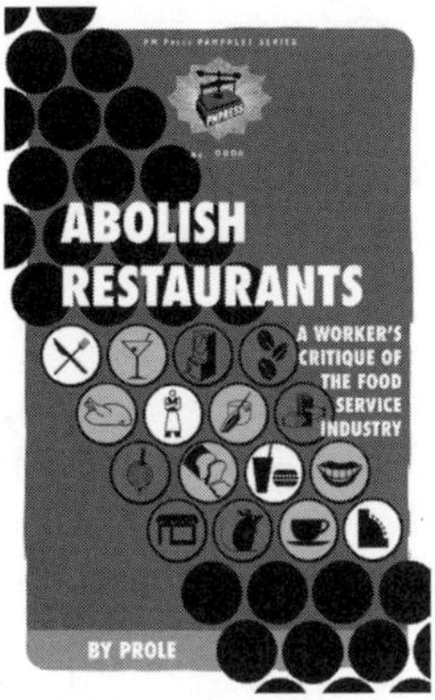
ABOLISH
RESTAURANTS
A WORKER'S
CRITIQUE OF
THE FOOD
SERVICE
INDUSTRY
BY PROLE

Abolish Restaurants

A Worker's Critique of the Food Service Industry

prole.info

ISBN: 978-1-60486-048-1 • $5.95

A 60-page illustrated guide to the daily misery, stress, boredom, and alienation of restaurant work, as well as the ways in which restaurant workers fight against it. Drawing on a range of anti-capitalist ideas as well as a heaping plate of personal experience, it is part analysis and part call-to-arms.

"Prole" is short for "proletarian," a word used by Karl Marx to describe the working class under capitalism. We are all the people in this society who do not own property or a business we can make money from, and therefore have to sell our time and energy to a boss—we are forced to work. Our work is the basis of this society.

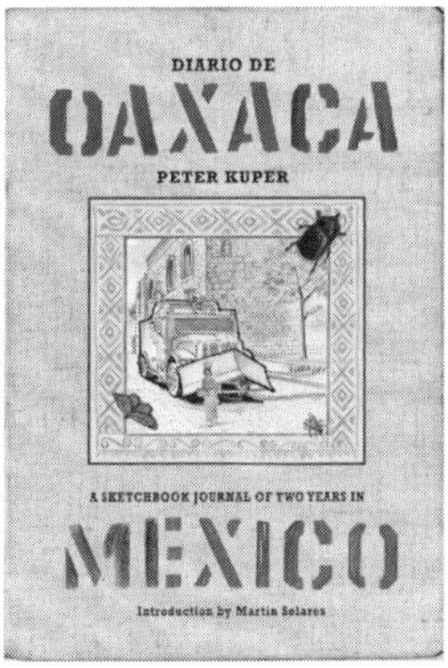
DIARIO DE
OAXACA
PETER KUPER
A SKETCHBOOK JOURNAL OF TWO YEARS IN
MEXICO
Introduction by Martin Solares

Diario De Oaxaca

A Sketchbook Journal of Two Years in Mexico

Peter Kuper

ISBN: 978-1-60486-071-9 • $29.95

Painting a vivid, personal portrait of social and political upheaval in Oaxaca, Mexico, this unique memoir employs comics, bilingual essays, photos, and sketches to chronicle the events that unfolded around a teachers' strike and led to a seven-month siege.

When award-winning cartoonist Peter Kuper and his wife and daughter moved to the beautiful 16th-century colonial town of Oaxaca in 2006, they planned to spend a quiet year or two enjoying a different culture and taking a break from the U.S. political climate under the Bush administration. What they hadn't counted on was landing in the epicenter of Mexico's biggest political struggle in recent years. Timely and compelling, this extraordinary firsthand account presents a distinct artistic vision of Oaxacan life, from explorations of the beauty of the environment to graphic portrayals of the fight between strikers and government troops that left more than 20 people dead, including American journalist Brad Will.

"Peter Kuper is undoubtedly the modern master whose work has refined the socially relevant comic to the highest point yet achieved." –Newsarama

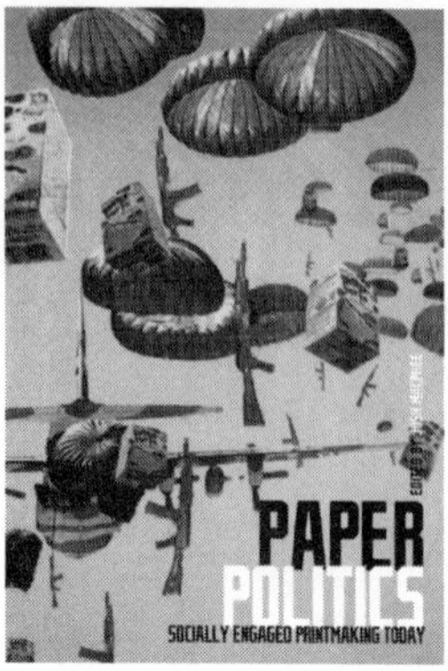
PAPER
POLITICS
SOCIALLY ENGAGED PRINTMAKING TODAY

Paper Politics

Socially Engaged Printmaking Today

Edited by Josh MacPhee

ISBN: 978-1-60486-090-0 • $24.95

Paper Politics: Socially Engaged Printmaking Today is a major collection of contemporary politically and socially engaged printmaking. This full-color book showcases print art that uses themes of social justice and global equity to engage community members in political conversation. Based on an art exhibition which has traveled to a dozen cities in North America, *Paper Politics* features artwork by over 200 international artists; an eclectic collection of work by both activist and non-activist printmakers who have felt the need to respond to the monumental trends and events of our times.

Paper Politics presents a breathtaking tour of the many modalities of printing by hand: relief, intaglio, lithography, serigraph, collagraph, monotype, and photography. In addition to these techniques, included are more traditional media used to convey political thought, finely crafted stencils and silk-screens intended for wheat pasting in the street. Artists range from the well established (Sue Coe, Swoon, Carlos Cortez) to the up-and-coming (Favianna Rodriguez, Chris Stain, Nicole Schulman), from street artists (BORF, You Are Beautiful) to rock poster makers (EMEK, Bughouse).

Josh MacPhee is a Brooklyn-based artist, curator, designer and activist currently living in Brooklyn, NY. His work often revolves around themes of radical politics, privatization and public space. He regularly produces posters and graphics for political groups and events, as well as to sell on Justseeds.org, a political art collective he helped found. He organizes the Celebrate People's History Poster Series and is often in front of his computer designing books for PM Press.

"Let's face it, most collections of activist art suck. Either esthetic concerns are front and center and the politics that motivate such creation are pushed to the margin, or politics prevail and artistic quality is an afterthought. With the heart of an activist and the eye of an artist, Josh MacPhee miraculously manages to do justice to both. Paper Politics *is singularly impressive." —Stephen Duncombe, author of* Dream: Re-Imagining Progressive Politics in an Age of Fantasy

"For all of those who claim that poster art is dead in the age of YouTube and Blogs, Paper Politics *will wheatpaste another message over your computer monitor. This exhibition and book is a testament to the vibrant trajectory of printmaking in the service of social change, including examples of earlier movements and artists as well as the graphics popping up right now. Obscure and familiar subjects are presented with wit, joy, and searing satire, guaranteed to snap your senses and challenge your opinions. It took a village to make this show, and the world will benefit from seeing it." —Lincoln Cushing, author of* Revolucion! Cuban Poster Art

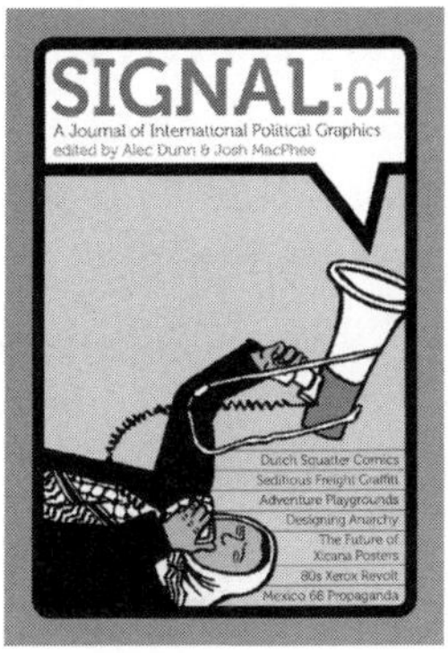
SIGNAL:01
A Journal of International Political Graphics
edited by Alec Dunn & Josh MacPhee
Dutch Squatter Comics
Seditious Freight Graffiti
Adventure Playgrounds
Designing Anarchy
The Future of Xicana Posters
80s Xerox Revolt
Mexico 68 Propaganda

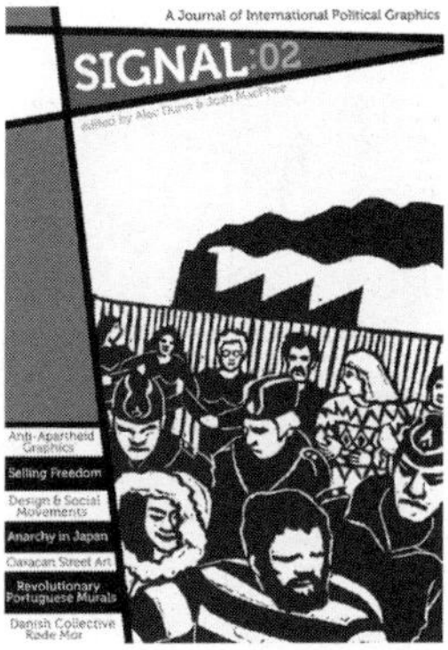
A Journal of International Political Graphics
SIGNAL:02
edited by Alec Dunn & Josh MacPhee
Anti-Apartheid Graphics
Selling Freedom
Design & Social Movements
Anarchy in Japan
Oaxacan Street Art
Revolutionary Portuguese Murals
Danish Collective Røde Mor

Signal: 01
A Journal of International Political Graphics
Edited by Josh MacPhee and Alec Icky Dunn
ISBN: 978-1-60486-091-7 • $14.95

Signal: 02
A Journal of International Political Graphics
Edited by Josh MacPhee and Alec Icky Dunn
ISBN: 978-1-60486-298-0 • $14.95

Signal is an ongoing book series dedicated to documenting and sharing compelling graphics, art projects, and cultural movements of international resistance and liberation struggles. Artists and cultural workers have been at the center of upheavals and revolts the world over, from the painters and poets in the Paris Commune to the poster makers and street theatre performers of the recent counter globalization movement. *Signal* will bring these artists and their work to a new audience, digging deep through our common history to unearth their images and stories. We have no doubt that *Signal* will come to serve as a unique and irreplaceable resource for activist artists and academic researchers, as well as an active forum for critique of the role of art in revolution.

In the U.S. there is a tendency to focus only on the artworks produced within our shores or from English speaking producers. *Signal* reaches beyond those bounds, bringing material produced the world over, translated from dozens of languages and collected from both the present and decades past. Though it is a full-color printed publication, *Signal* is not limited to the graphic arts. Within its pages you will find political posters and fine arts, comics and murals, street art, site specific works, zines, art collectives, documentation of performance and articles on the often overlooked but essential role all of these have played in struggles around the world.

> "Signal *is dotted with stunning photography that will certainly reel in many people who are into unusual art. Clocking in at just under 140 glossy pages, Dunn and MacPhee do an impressive job of conveying not only what is new and relevant in political art, but also its history and its presence in the everyday."* —Political Media Review

BANKSY
LOCATIONS & TOURS
VOL 1
A COLLECTION OF GRAFFITI LOCATIONS AND PHOTOGRAPHS IN LONDON, ENGLAND
BY MARTIN BULL
US EDITION
REVISED & EXPANDED

Banksy Location and Tours Volume 1
A Collection of Graffiti Locations and Photographs in London, England
Edited by Martin Bull
ISBN: 978-1-60486-320-8 • $20.00

When it comes to art, London is best known for its galleries, not its graffiti. However, not if photographer Martin Bull has anything to say about it. While newspapers and magazines the world over send their critics to review the latest Damien Hirst show at the Tate Modern, Bull, in turn, is out taking photos of the latest street installations by guerilla art icon Banksy.

In three guided tours, Martin Bull documents sixty-five London sites where one can see some of the most important works by the legendary political artist. Boasting over 100 color photos, *Banksy Locations and Tours Volume 1* also includes graffiti by many of Banksy's peers, including Eine, Faile, El Chivo, Arofish, Cept, Space Invader, Blek Le Rat, D*face, and Shepherd Fairey.

US EDITION
BY MARTIN BULL
BANKSY
LOCATIONS & TOURS VOL 2
A COLLECTION OF GRAFFITI LOCATIONS AND PHOTOGRAPHS FROM AROUND THE UK

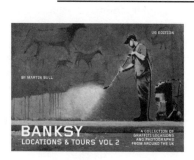

Banksy Locations and Tours Volume 2
A Collection of Graffiti Locations and Photographs from around the UK
Edited by Martin Bull
ISBN: 978-1-60486-330-7 • $20.00

This unique and unashamedly DIY book follows the runaway success of *Banksy Locations and Tours Vol. 1* by rounding up the rest of Banksy's UK graffiti from the last five years. It includes over 100 different locations and 200 color photographs of Banksy's street art; information, random facts, and idle chit-chat on each location; a full walking tour of his remaining work in Bristol, England; and snippets of graffiti by several other artists.

Visit the locations in-person, or get your slippers on and settle back for an open-top bus ride though some of Banksy's best public work.

> *"Martin Bull charts the mysterious appearances—and sadly, sloppy destruction—of Banksy graffiti all over London, complete with maps and notes on the present condition of his works. Bull's unpretentious style and dedication to graffiti art comes across in everything he writes."* —London Sketchbook *on* Volume 1

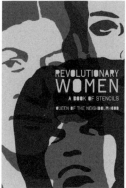

REVOLUTIONARY
WOMEN
A BOOK OF STENCILS
QUEEN OF THE NEIGHBOURHOOD

Revolutionary Women

A Book of Stencils

Queen of the Neighbourhood

ISBN: 978-1-60486-200-3 • $12.00

A radical feminist history and street art resource for inspired readers! This book combines short biographies with striking and usable stencil images of thirty women—activists, anarchists, feminists, freedom-fighters and visionaries.

It offers a subversive portrait history which refuses to belittle the military prowess and revolutionary drive of women, whose violent resolves often shatter the archetype of woman-as-nurturer. It is also a celebration of some extremely brave women who have spent their lives fighting for what they believe in and rallying supporters in climates where a woman's authority is never taken as seriously as a man's. The text also shares some of each woman's ideologies, philosophies, struggles and quiet humanity with quotes from their writings or speeches.

THE REAL
COST OF
PRISONS
COMIX

The Real Cost of Prisons Comix

Edited by Lois Ahrens

ISBN: 978-1-60486-034-4 • $14.95

Winner of the 2008 PASS Award (Prevention for a Safer Society) from the National Council on Crime and Delinquency

One out of every hundred adults in the U.S. is in prison. This book provides a crash course in what drives mass incarceration, the human and community costs, and how to stop the numbers from going even higher. This volume collects the three comic books published by the Real Cost of Prisons Project. The stories and statistical information in each comic book is thoroughly researched and documented.

The comics included in the collection are: "Prison Town: Paying the Price," "Prisoners of the War on Drugs," and "Prisoners of a Hard Life: Women and Their Children.

Also included are alternatives to the present system, a glossary and footnotes.

"I cannot think of a better way to arouse the public to the cruelties of the prison system than to make this book widely available." —Howard Zinn

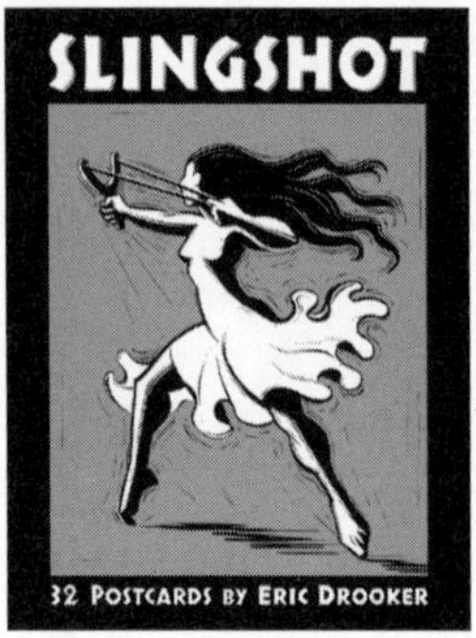
SLINGSHOT
32 POSTCARDS BY ERIC DROOKER

Slingshot

32 Postcards

Eric Drooker

ISBN: 978-1-60486-016-0 • $14.95

Disguised as a book of innocent postcards, *Slingshot* is a dangerous collection of Eric Drooker's most notorious posters. Plastered on brick walls from New York to Berlin, tattooed on bodies from Kansas to Mexico City, Drooker's graphics continue to infiltrate and inflame the body politic. Drooker is the author of two graphic novels, *Flood! A Novel in Pictures*, and *Blood Song: A Silent Ballad*. He collaborated with Beat poet Allen Ginsberg on the underground classic *Illuminated Poems*. His provocative art has appeared on countless posters, book and CD covers, and his hard-edged graphics are a familiar sight on street corners throughout the world.

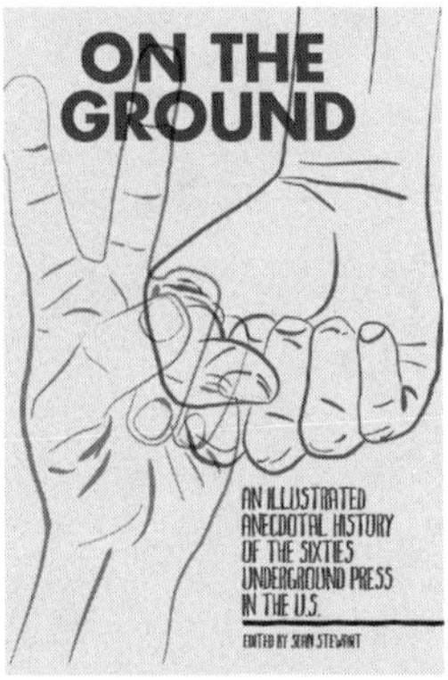
ON THE GROUND
AN ILLUSTRATED ANECDOTAL HISTORY OF THE SIXTIES UNDERGROUND PRESS IN THE U.S.

On the Ground

An Illustrated Anecdotal History of the Sixties Underground Press in the U.S.

Edited by Sean Stewart

ISBN: 978-1-60486-455-7 • $20.00

In four short years (1965–1969), the underground press grew from five small newspapers in as many cities in the U.S. to over 500 newspapers—with millions of readers—all over the world. Completely circumventing (and subverting) establishment media by utilizing their own news service and freely sharing content amongst each other, the underground press, at its height, became the unifying institution for the counterculture of the 1960s.

Frustrated with the lack of any mainstream media criticism of the Vietnam War, empowered by the victories of the Civil Rights era, emboldened by the anti-colonial movements in the third world and with heads full of acid, a generation set out to change the world. The underground press was there documenting, participating in, and providing the resources that would guarantee the growth of this emergent youth culture.

Neither meant to be an official nor comprehensive history, *On the Ground* focuses on the anecdotal detail that brings the history alive. Composed of stories told by the people involved with the production and distribution of the newspapers and featuring over 50 full-color scans taken from a broad range of newspapers, the book provides a true window into the spirit of the times, giving the reader a feeling for the energy on the ground.